If Only I Had Known

If Only I Had Known

Dramatic Monologues
for Advent and Lent

David P. Polk

Chalice Press
St. Louis, Missouri

Scripture quotations not otherwise designated are from the *New Revised Standard Version Bible*, copyright 1989, Division of Christian Education of the National Council of the Churches of Christ in the USA and are used by permission.

Permission is granted for the dramatic presentation of these monologues, provided that no admission fee is charged, due credit is given to the author, and one copy of this book is purchased for use by the presenter.

Cover and illustrations: Glenn Myers

Art director: Michael Dominguez

10 9 8 7 6 5 4 3 2 1

Library of Congress Cataloging–in–Publication Data

(pending)

Printed in the United States of America

To my wife, Kitty,
and to the members of
First Christian Church,
Cedar Rapids, Iowa,
who first welcomed these visitors
into their lives

Contents

Introduction

The innkeeper of Bethlehem is a much maligned fellow in our depictions of the Savior's birth. After all, how could he have been so callous? Didn't he know who these special guests were? Some men of wisdom from faraway Persia trekked hundreds of miles to greet the newly born babe, and they weren't even Hebrews. So where does this lowlife proprietor come off, being so rude? In a melodrama, he would be sporting a waxed handlebar mustache and we would boo and hiss him when he came on stage.

But hold on a moment. Are we playing fair here? The inn, after all, was full. Whom was he going to displace? Besides, Joseph kept receiving holy dreams. The hapless innkeeper wasn't allowed in on the plot.

1

He didn't even get an angelic chorus to clue him in on the extraordinary events taking place out in his stable. So how was he to know?

There is another, often overlooked little detail. That is the fact that we ourselves have conjured up this nameless innkeeper in the first place. Check it out. No innkeeper is mentioned in Luke's account of the nativity. One finds simply the brief, poignant observation, "there was no place for them in the inn" (Luke 2:7).

Ah, the human imagination! What a rich and powerful role it plays in our spiritual life. The innkeeper doesn't exactly exist in scripture and so we invent him—as a minor villain to go along with that major villain Herod and, later, Pontius Pilate and those other men-in-power.

This collection of vivid first-person narratives is an extension of that wonderful God-given gift called the imagination. I invite you to immerse yourself imaginatively into the scenes of Jesus' birth and death by means of these dramatizations. They do not claim to be anything more than this. But that does not render them any the less rewarding. A good deal of research lies behind the tellings, but I try to let it stay in the background. What I present are ten "eyewitness" accounts, a recounting of "how it might have been." If the stories move you to reflect and ponder, and perhaps to see with a new kind of clarity, they will have served their purpose.

The jumping-off point for this spiritual excursion was my growing frustration that we tend to frontload the Jesus story with too much weight on the nativity scene itself. I mean, here are all these singing angels and heavenly messengers and gift-bearing Magi all over the place, so the meaning of the drama has to be clear to everyone from the beginning. Right?

Wrong. With the exception of some singular experiences shared only by a tiny few, the one destined to be God's incarnate presence among us was born into obscurity and vulnerability. Christmas doesn't tell its story by itself. By itself, Christmas doesn't have a story to tell. We have to read the lines backward. Only by the light of Easter is the perplexing manger scene truly illuminated.

And so the embarrassed innkeeper can rightly bemoan, "If only I had known who was seeking shelter in my establishment." But did the shepherds *really* know what the heavenly announcement was all about as they huddled in amazement around the fragile infant in the feed box? Had the Magi any inkling of the kind of king they were welcoming into the world?

It continued to be mystifying, right down to the end. What *really* motivated Judas to turn in his best friend to the authorities? Why was the Roman centurion so strangely moved? Could Barabbas appreciate the gift of the one whose execution gave him an undeserved reprieve?

I have painted these individuals with sympathetic tones, for the most part. Pilate is the singular exception—but even in his unrepentant posturing he has an important statement to make to those of us who claim to follow the one he put to death. Several are allowed the passage of time to bring their stories to imagined completeness (Nathan the shepherd, Simon of Cyrene, Senecus the centurion).

Jesus is, of course, the consistent focus of these musings. Unlike the ten "narrators," I have been unable to put words into his mouth that are not already present in the Gospels. But if he speaks directly only very little, his striking presence predominates throughout.

Ten different individuals see him in very different ways, but there is one striking constant—*the eyes*! I have tried to imagine what it could have been like to have been in Jesus' physical presence. The one prevailing characteristic that always bears in on me is the sense that those eyes must have been electrifying. If the eyes are the mirror of the soul, Jesus' eyes were surely no less than the mirror of the Divine.

I am sharing with you these imaginary stories of ten men who encountered Jesus. Yes, they are, in fact, all men. That is because I find I cannot faithfully leap over the gender gap to imagine with any integrity how women might have reacted to him. I await with eager anticipation a woman's fresh telling of those women's stories.

These narratives originally came into existence in the form of "dramatic monologues" delivered from a pulpit during the seasons of Advent and Lent. Their number exactly corresponds with the Sundays of those two seasons of the church year. Though I believe their usefulness extends beyond that format, some may wish to offer these as dramatic readings in a church setting. In support of that, I am providing a set of brief performance notes at the end of the book.

Call Me

Ahkmet

Innkeeper

(Luke 2:1–7)

Look, I'm terribly sorry, really I am. I just didn't know, didn't realize who they were. How could I have been expected to know?

Oh. I beg your pardon. We haven't been properly introduced. Excuse me for going on like that but...well, I guess I do get rather defensive about the whole affair.

You may call me Ahkmet. Innkeeper, by profession. Uh, not just any innkeeper....I'm *that* innkeeper. You know, the one from Bethlehem.

Yes, I'm the ogre you all think so horribly of. I was there on that fateful night, when the heavens opened up and God touched the earth with the gentle beauty of a child of love.

I'm the one who had the colossal stupidity, the blind callousness, to shut the door in their tired, hungry faces. I said, "No, I'm sorry, I have no more room"—and I've been extremely uncomfortable about it ever since.

Let me tell you about it—no, not to excuse myself, not to gain your pity. Let me tell you my story so that perhaps you might learn from my mistake and not repeat it. And, maybe, in so doing, I might even help you realize a bit more fully what that remarkable night was really all about.

It's not all that much of an establishment, to tell the truth. But it has stood well the test of time. I inherited it from my father, just as it was handed down to him by his father. The inn has been in our family for many generations.

There is only this one inn, you see. Bethlehem is nothing more than a large village—but a very proud village, you can be sure of that. Remember, this is the town that spawned the great King David. We've never forgotten that. But, well, we've been living mostly with memories for a long time now. Several hundred townsfolk are all who live here—except for the rainy season when the shepherds congregate here while their flocks graze nearby. Then, maybe a thousand at most.

But I'm not putting it down, oh no. It's really very pleasant around here. The land is amazingly fertile in this vicinity. You know, right south of us is the barren wilderness of the Negeb, and to the east lies the Dead Sea. But here, around Bethlehem, the fig trees and the olive groves are abundant, the wheat grows tall and full, the sheep find plenty of grazing pasture. Why, do you know what the name means, "Bethlehem"? No? It means "house of bread."

House of bread. House of plenty. Would that my inn could be called that. But alas, it's never been all that lucrative a business. Jerusalem is only two hours away on foot, you know. Why spend the night in Bethlehem when you might as well trek on up to the holy city where the rooms are more abundant and the inns are finer?

Mine is but a small caravansary. It's a place where the traders can pen their camels and get a warm meal and a roof over their heads before they head off to the next village. And the nomadic herdsmen come into town from time to time, to buy grain, and to sell their woven cloth and goat's cheese in the Bethlehem marketplace. That's about the pace of it. If it were not for my own small herd of goats and a few dozen sheep, I'm sure I would not be able to keep my head above water at all.

There was that one time, though, when business was really booming. They came and they came and they just kept on coming. The Romans were the cause of it all—curse their evil hides! Well, sure they were bringing me more business—more, in fact, than I could handle. But do you know what it's like, living under foreign overlords? The insults you have to accept, without so much as a clenched fist? The fear that bears down on you, even in your bed at night—never certain but that armed soldiers might suddenly be beating on your door, coming to cart you away for some trumped-up infraction? And the taxes—ach, the taxes! The greedy dogs, they never seem to bleed us enough.

It was the system of Roman taxation that kept bringing me all that flood of business, filling my small caravansary night after night to overflowing. People were arriving from miles around to register their property rights with the Roman authorities and protect them from overassessment—or even outright seizure. Anyone who held any title to any lands in the Bethlehem area, or any portion of any lands, or could claim the right of inheritance to any lands, had to come to have their claims duly entered in the Roman ledgers. And to what purpose? Why, for more taxes, what else!

Strange, how that one particular night has clung so tenaciously in my memory. Because it was not until so many years later that I really learned what that night had signified. But the face of that man…pleading softly with his eyes into my own, looking so achingly vulnerable.

It was incredibly hectic, with my wife and daughter trying desperately to prepare and serve food for everyone, all those people crowded together in a place intended for half so many. And then he was there, quietly in the midst of the noisy chaos, soliciting my attention. "Innkeeper," he asked, "have you a room for my wife and me?"

Very simply put. No pleading—no, uh, jingling of coin to suggest I "find" a bit of room by displacing someone else. But couldn't he see what he was up against? Couldn't he see the impossibility of the situation staring him right in the face?

I'm afraid I was rather brusque with the man. My "No!" had a ring of finality about it. Well, after all, it was ridiculously late for someone to come strolling in at that hour and expect to find some unoccupied niche in which to lay his head. There just wasn't any and that was that.

I was standing near the open doorway, and I happened to glance momentarily out into the courtyard as he was leaving. That's when I saw her. She looked so young, and so fragile, sitting on the donkey—and so very weary. But there was something else that made me look again: beneath the wraps that protected her from the chilly night air, it was apparent to me that the young woman was, well, very far along in pregnancy. Her time of delivery could not be very far off, a few days or weeks at the most, I thought.

I hadn't expected that. He was standing there beside the donkey, talking to her—explaining their dilemma, no doubt. A flash of light from the fire in the courtyard caught her face, and I saw that she was hardly more than a girl, barely fifteen or so—though the man who had spoken to me was somewhat older.

I don't know what made me think of it—some flash of inspiration that just comes without warning. He had already taken the donkey by his harness and was leading him out of the courtyard when I impulsively bolted from the doorway and yelled after them to stop.

"Wait!" I said. "Where are you going? You can't find a place to stay at this hour. Bethlehem's packed."

He made a motion that seemed to say they'd bed down under the stars. "But the nights get rather cold, up here in the hill country," I told him. "And in her condition...." I didn't need to finish. We both knew what I meant.

"Look," I said, "I know it isn't much, but it's warm, and it's clean. Right over there, the cave, where I stable my animals when it rains. There's plenty of fresh straw for beds." I stopped, and shrugged my shoulders in a gesture of helpless resignation.

The young woman looked at her husband with a spirit of calm that belied her predicament and gently nodded her head. It would do.

I took a few moments to make sure they got settled. "You're Galilean, aren't you?" I ventured. "I can tell by your appearance and dress." He acknowledged that he was. From Nazareth, in fact. A carpenter by trade. "Four days' journey?" I pondered aloud. No wonder so weary. "Five," said he— "because of my wife's condition."

"Call me Ahkmet," I said, refusing to accept the coin he held out in payment for the night's lodging in a lowly stable.

"I am Joseph," said he, adding with a quiet dignity: "of the house of David. And this is my wife, Mary."

The night passed with the usual clamor of an overcrowded inn. The animals out in the courtyard seemed to be stirring about more than was their habit, but not so much as to rouse my curiosity. It was not until the middle of the next morning, during a brief lull in the flurry of responsibility that is an innkeeper's lot, that I again thought of them. On an impulse, I decided to check in on them. Probably they would have left by now, using the daylight hours to find a more suitable lodging with one of the town's families, a distant relative perhaps.

But no, they were still there, and the sight that greeted my eyes in the dim half-light of the cave caused me to tremble with astonishment.

They had been two. Now they were three!

It was really very touching. She had prepared a crib for him by using the feed box—the manger, layered with straw. He was lying there, radiating such utter contentment. I simply had to smile.

"What will you call him?" I asked.

"Jesus," they told me.

Jesus, I thought. A common enough name—the same, really, as "Joshua." I pondered its meaning for a moment: "God will save."

It meant little enough to me then. It was just another baby, suddeny thrust upon a world all too cruel for the trusting innocence of a helpless infant. I laughed inwardly, bitterly, at the irony of it: a baby named "God will save," born in my rock-hewn stable.

I could hardly leave them there. And the crowded conditions of my inn were no fair haven for a day-old infant. We managed to locate a spare room for them in one of the smaller houses in the town. I never saw them again after that.

So you're wondering why I've continued to hold the memory of that night in my mind ever since? Curiosity, perhaps? It's not every night that you have a baby born in your stable. But something more. The radiant calm of that Galilean couple, the way their very presence made me feel, for the moment, somehow different. Don't ask me to explain. I can't. I just never forgot, that's all.

That's why I was finally able to put the pieces together, years later—because I couldn't forget. When the buzz reached Bethlehem about the strange and exciting preacher that some called prophet and some dared call Messiah, I ignored it at first. I was an old man by then. We had long expected our messiah to come and save us, and every time one seemed to appear on the scene, he turned out to be nothing but a brave though misguided man. Always the hopes were for naught.

This one's name was Jesus. *So what?* I thought. A common enough name for a messiah. Then I heard the phrase that sent a chill coursing through my weary bones: "Jesus of Nazareth." And the memory of that night came flooding back with all the intensity of a yesterday. They were from Nazareth! And the age...was right.

The words of one of our prophets, Micah, cut through me like a sword—words I had long scoffed at, ignored without a second thought: "But you, O

Bethlehem of Ephrathah, who are one of the little clans of Judah, from you shall come forth for me one who is to rule in Israel....And he shall stand and feed his flock in the strength of the LORD, in the majesty of the name of the LORD his God. And they shall live secure, for now he shall be great to the ends of the earth..." (5:2, 4).

I have lived long enough now to realize that this time, he has really come. And I have lived to experience the shame, the foolhardiness of my actions on the eventful night long ago when I had my one great opportunity and failed. Out of blindness, insensitivity, I turned them away from my door; I was willing only to afford them the comforts I reserved for my *animals*.

Oh, I had other alternatives; I realize that now. I could have moved my family and me into that cave, and given them our room. But *I didn't know*. I didn't know who they were—how could I have known?

I have heard his message secondhand, and I have gained some solace from it. For into the guilt I feel over having turned the Savior of us all away at my door comes his soothing assurance of forgiveness. And what lies behind that unmerited gift of forgiveness has helped me see more clearly what my blunder was really all about.

I realize now—that I was guilty for failing to expect the unexpected! In the familiar routine that marked my life, I was not open to the sudden inbreaking of God's unpredictable call, God's offer, God's grace.

I realize now—that I was guilty of not being able to give except when I could find some earthly, sensible reason for giving. I demanded to know in advance what my act of giving would be for. I could not simply give for the beauty of giving, love in the joy of love itself.

He has taught me that. "If only I could have known!" I cried. But even as he forgave my blindness he has punctured the pretense of my excuses. For now I know that to turn *any* needy traveler away from my inn is to turn *him* away.

It happened right under my nose, the birth of God's Messiah, and I could offer nothing better than a stable in a cave.

It's your turn now. What do you offer?

Is there any room in *you* for his arrival?

Call Me
Nathan
Shepherd

(Luke 2:8–20)

H i. I don't feel right, being here. I'm kind of nervous.

I mean...I'm not good with words; I haven't had a lot of schooling. I can't make a fancy, eloquent speech. I'm afraid you'll find me, uh, rather ordinary.

But *he* was that way too. Oh no, I don't mean he was *ordinary*. But he spoke words that I could understand—simple, right to the point. That's the amazing thing—that he spoke *my* language, *me*, Nathan: a mere shepherd. He was always being pestered with complicated questions by those learned scribes and other smart alecks—and yet when he answered them, it was in a way people like me could understand. And when he talked about sheep, about being a shepherd himself, I really liked that. I could get the sense of it real clear.

Oh, but see—there I go already, getting all ahead of my story. Forgive me, please. I'm not used to standing up in front of a lot of people and talking. Like I said, I'm a shepherd. I spend my time in the company of sheep and a handful of other herdsmen like myself. I'm not much for big crowds. I like being out by myself, under the canopy of stars, watching over my flock—or sitting around the fire talking with my shepherd friends.

That's what we were doing that night when the heavens suddenly burst open all around us and we were so totally dumbfounded by the strange mystery of it all.

I was only a lad of twelve at the time, the youngest of our small shepherd band. It had not been very many months that my father had let me go with him and the others into the high pasturelands and actually stay all the time with them and the grazing sheep. But I was learning fast, and more than once I had rescued a careless lamb from a thicket of brambles and retrieved others that had strayed too far from the flock. Already they were letting me stand watch by myself some nights against the threat of marauders and animals of prey. They trusted me—little Nathan!

I was happy about that. Sheep are so utterly vulnerable, you know. They're completely defenseless by themselves. They are totally dependent on us shepherds for everything—protecting them, finding them fresh water and green pastures, making sure they don't wander off and get lost. It was really an honor that my elders would entrust the care of their flocks to me once in a while.

That night—that fantastic, unforgettable night—it was my turn to stay up on watch. But we were still all sitting around the dying fire, talking quietly. I listened, of course, out of respect for my elders—and out of interest, too. They were forever sharing with each other the exciting stories of our ancestors in the days of our people's greatness. They talked about King David and King Solomon, about the great lawgiver Moses, about our ancient ancestors Abraham and Sarah.

Much of the time, the conversation turned with pride around the great tradition of shepherding among our people. We weren't all that respected any more—we were pretty much on the fringes of society, and were looked down upon by the more well-off who dwelled in the towns and cities. But I could beam with pride when I heard the stories of the patriarchs, who had been herdsman, and of Moses, who was tending his father-in-law's flocks when God called him to go lead our people out of slavery. And the marvel of David, the shepherd boy who became king! That was really thrilling. And the prophets had talked about Israel as sheep and God as the great Shepherd who would lead us all back into God's sheepfold and tenderly care for us. I never tired of hearing about that.

But there I go again, getting off the track. You want to hear about that night of nights. OK.

There was a strange stirring in the air, I remember that. The sheep sensed it—they were unusually restless. I wondered if there was possibly a pack of wild animals in the area.

But then the light exploded upon us, and all thought of natural enemies disappeared from my head. My father stopped in mid-sentence; we all froze with unspeakable terror. I was sure the world was coming to an end, right then and there. Our prophets had said that at the close of the age, the glory of the Lord Yahweh would be disclosed. This brilliant light that shone like the brightest day but had no visible source—this was surely the glory of God, and the end was at hand.

But as I trembled in my panic, I became aware of something else—sounds, soft and gentle, coming from everywhere and yet nowhere. And then the sounds filled me with a sense of the most wondrous strains of music, flooding my soul like a thousand tumbling waterfalls. I felt so perfectly at peace.

Then it was over. Gone. We looked into each other's faces and knew we hadn't just imagined it. Then the silence among us was shattered all in a rush. Words tumbling out, breathlessly—"Did you hear it?" "Yes, a message, from Heaven." "The Messiah is being born. Tonight." "Down in Bethlehem, King David's city." "Yes, I heard that too—I'm sure I did."

It was amazing. We were discovering that we had all received the same impression of a message, even though I wasn't aware of hearing any words. I was confused and excited and happy all at the same time.

Suddenly I sensed that something was out of place. The sheep! I turned my head around to where the flocks were gathered. The sight made no sense: they were perfectly calm—as though nothing had just happened at all. They had not bolted in fear—had not even roused.

The men were sharing their bewilderment over something else they thought they had heard. "God's deliverer, lying in a manger? In a common feed trough? That's ridiculous!" "Yes, but we all heard the same thing. We're sure we did."

I had the same impression, and it made no sense to me either. Had we simply dreamed all this? And the sheep—the way they were so completely unaware...?

But we were all filled with extreme curiosity—and no one more than I. The trek into Bethlehem...would be made. Something this puzzling could not be ignored.

I sprung to my feet, overflowing with excitement. Only then did I remember: it was *my* night to keep watch. The sheep could not be left alone. Someone would have to remain behind—and that someone was me. My one chance to see the wonder of the ages would be denied me.

I was staring down at the ground, shuffling my feet in dismay, as they started off. Then I heard the voice of Simeon, the eldest, close beside me—and I remember his words so clearly:

"Go ahead, little Nathan. Go with them. I'm old, and full of life already. You're young—you have your life before you. The coming of God's Messiah will mean a great deal to you in the years ahead. Go. I'll tend the sheep. You come back and tell me about it—let me see it through your eyes."

Impulsively I hugged the kind old shepherd, then ran to catch up with the others. They were walking fast, in a hurry to cut through the veil of mystery that enveloped this night. I walked beside my father and told him about Simeon's insistence that I go in his place, and he showed his pleasure with a smile and a nod.

I wondered to myself, as we approached the sleeping village, how the men would know where to find this manger with its surprising occupant. Would the Savior of our people really come into the world in a *stable*, of all places?!

It was strange. We wandered through the darkened streets in silence, and yet we didn't really seem to be wandering at all. No one said, "Let's try the inn." We just eventually wound up there, in the courtyard—and saw the unmistakable glow of candlelight coming from one of the grottoes where the animals were bedded down. Of course, it could have been anyone, since the inn was obviously so full. We rushed excitedly to the entrance of the cave, and peered in.

I was behind the others, and could not see very well around them. But I could make out the face of a man, who looked as puzzled as we. And over by the feed box, a girl not much older than I. A chill went down my spine as I realized that the manger held a tiny newborn baby!

We just stood there, quietly staring. The man asked why we'd come, what we wanted. And the words came pouring out, from my father and the others too. About the strange vision of the light, and the sense of a message about the Messiah being born this very night, here in Bethlehem, and the sign being a baby lying in a manger. The man looked bewildered. But I saw the young woman smile softly, and I heard her ask her husband to let us come inside and see her infant son.We crowded around the three of them, in quiet awe. He seemed to me to be so ordinary—and so totally vulnerable. *Is God playing a joke on us?* I thought to myself. I tell you, I no more understood what was taking place than…than those sheep up there on the hillside. None of it made any sense to me, not then—not really.

Later that night, when I shared everything with dear old Simeon—including my utter confusion—he smiled and put his hand gently on my shoulder. "Some day, little Nathan," he said, "you will find out what it means. And when you do, it will make your heart glad to have been a part of this remarkable night."

He was right, you know. I did learn to make some sense of it, though it was a long time in coming.

At first, we tried to tell everybody we saw—about the events of that night. But they laughed at us, and mocked us. No one else seemed to have noticed anything unusual—except for the rumors about the strange men from some foreign land who had been seen in the town several days afterward. No, everything was still the same. The Romans still oppressed us. Our own leaders abused us. The night of wonder had made no difference at all. Gradually my youthful excitement cooled, until I convinced myself it had all been a foolish, confused mistake.

Almost. Almost convinced myself. Always the nagging feeling deep inside, that it had not been a deception, or a mirage—that would not totally go away.

I stayed with the flocks, at peace with myself in the simple, somewhat solitary life of the shepherd. The years passed, and many more claimants for the role of messiah came and went, and many more hopes were dashed. And then I began to hear about a man from up north, from Galilee, who was attracting big crowds with his preaching. What I heard about him stirred up something inside of me, for they said he was a man who went around in the company of life's losers—the poor, the maimed, the abused, the outcasts. They said his closest followers were fishermen and people like that—people like me. Ordinary people.

Once again, curiosity seized me tightly in its grip. Moses had turned aside from his flocks to see a burning bush. I had turned aside once, and was left bewildered and confused. I decided I would make one more try.

I left the sheep in the care of my own grown sons and journeyed north, to Galilee. It wasn't hard to find him, for many were the persons who knew of him. But when I caught up with him, I was filled with a sense of disappointment all over again. This man, Jesus from Nazareth, couldn't be the Messiah. He looked so unimposing, so ragtag. He looked...strangely vulnerable—like that tiny baby in its makeshift crib that night in Bethlehem.

It was this haunting similarity that compelled me to follow him around for several weeks, listening and watching. And as I did so, I lost all my regrets for traveling so far—lost my lingering doubts about the importance of the night of wonder.

I told you, did I not? That he spoke in words that even I, a shepherd, could understand? And when he spoke, he seemed to be speaking directly to me—I've never gotten over the strangeness of that.

He talked about a shepherd going out to find the one lamb lost from the fold, and bringing it back safely. And I thought about our prophet Isaiah's words: *we are like sheep who have gone astray* (53:6). He told us of a shepherd's loyalty to his flock, and reminded us that a shepherd would even put his own life in jeopardy out of care and concern for his sheep. I knew about that.

I trembled inside: what an astonishing role for a Messiah—to be a shepherd! Again, Isaiah had spoken words like that: "He will feed his flock like a shepherd; he will gather the lambs in his arms, and carry them in his bosom, and gently lead the mother sheep" (40:11).

Yes, he would do that, I thought. A confusing notion went through my head—maybe you can make sense of it: David was a shepherd who became a king; this Jesus was going to be a king by becoming a shepherd!

I left him and went back to my beloved Bethlehem hills, and my family and my own shepherding responsibilities. But I went with a new gleam in my eye, for the sense of it was beginning to become clear:

He had been born in a lowly stable because his purpose was to lift up the lowly and the commonplace things of this world and let us see the beauty of them.

The message of his arrival had come to a handful of lowly shepherds because his messiahship was meant for people like us—common, ordinary people who don't pretend to be wise or secure or perfect. And we listened. In our simplicity and bewilderment, we heard.

We didn't understand—but we went and saw, even in our lack of understanding.

And then one more strange thought flooded into my mind.

Old Simeon had not gone to see, had let me go instead. He had sacrificed, on my behalf. And in that simple act of self-denial, I now knew, he had expressed what the Messiah's birth was really all about.

Call Me
Melchior
of the Magi

(Matthew 2:1–12)

Y ou may call me Melchior, of the Magi, if you please.
I understand I have been preceded in this place of
honor by other men who shared with you their remi-
niscences of the coming of your Lord and King. And I
understand that they confessed to you their lack of full
comprehension of that event of the ages. Do not expect
other of me.

Ah yes, I know I am called "wise man." I know that
I and my two companions were privileged to bestow
gifts upon the newborn king and pay him respectful
homage. And it is true that we traveled many weeks
over much harsh terrain to accomplish that purpose.

But do not give us glory that we do not deserve. Do
not be misled by the amazing scope of our worldly
wisdom. For the wisdom of God makes foolishness out

of our pretensions of great knowledge. We went, intending to offer our tribute to a king. Little did we realize the true nature of his kingship as it would come to be—no, not even we. Not even we.

I am from the city of Ecbatana in Media, in the mountains far to the east of the Tigris and the Euphrates. Our land is now ruled by the Parthians, but we still adhere to the faith of our Persian forebears, which you call Zoroastrianism. We who are Magi are the priests of our religion. Somehow you have gained the impression that my companions and I are kings, but that is utterly mistaken. We exercise authority only in the spiritual realm among our people.

Our responsibility goes much deeper than the performance of sacred ritual. We struggle to make sense out of the mysterious, so that our people may walk in the path of a higher truth. We study many things in our efforts to penetrate the mysteries of the cosmos. To that end, we have become skilled in the arts of what you call magic;* we are masters in the interpretation of dreams; and we scan the night sky, charting diligently the movements of the stars.

I recall so vividly the night that set me forth on the quest of my lifetime. For weeks in the spring of the year, I had been watching in growing anticipation as two great lights in the sky, appearing above the horizon shortly before midnight each night, seemed to be slowly converging. Balthasar and Caspar, my fellow Magi, shared my great excitement at this celestial occurrence. The three of us were there together on the level rooftop of my villa, conversing anxiously in hushed tones as we waited, with the city of Ecbatana

---

* The English word *magic* is derived from precisely this source, "Magi."

lying quietly beneath us in the darkness, and the sky above us ablaze with a thousand thousand lights. If our calculations were correct, this was the night we were awaiting.

We were heirs, you see, to the wondrous knowledge that every human being has a heavenly counterpart, a "fravashi," that appears as a star in the sky. The brighter the star, the greater the person will be whose coming the fravashi heralds. These two lights about to become one** were surely the sign of the imminent birth of a person of unparalleled greatness, one destined to achieve dominion over the lives of many.

As the middle of the night drew near, we watched in breathless awe as the two lights appeared anew on the distant horizon and began their climb. Then, with an amazing suddenness that made us gasp, the two glowing embers merged into one brilliant burst of blue-white fire, shimmering in the vault of heaven like a priceless diamond. Time held no meaning for us as we stared in speechless wonder at the dazzling sight. It was high in the eastern sky before Balthasar broke the silence with the words we were all feeling: "It is the sign. A king like none other will soon be born."

But where? And to whom? We had been excitedly pouring over the wisdom of the ages in search of that information, but without success. Now we redoubled our efforts with even greater enthusiasm and urgency. The thought of possessing this knowledge and not being able to act upon it was numbing. We would *have* to discover the location of his appearing, that we might go and render him the homage that was his due.

** It is a matter of astronomical record that in the year 7 B.C., Saturn and Jupiter converged and shone as one light over a period of several months. This has been advanced as one possible explanation of the "Star of the East." Incidentally, the conjunction also occurred as recently as 1981, but will not happen again until the year 2238.

We did not limit our searching to the prophetic traditions in our own sacred literature, and that was fortunate. One evening, nearly a month after the star had first ascended as a single blaze of light, Caspar came rushing into my house with remarkable news. "I have found it!" he exclaimed. "In the ancient books of the Hebrews."

"The Hebrews?" I replied in astonishment. "But they are of such undeniable insignificance as the affairs of this world go. They have been subjugated again and again, by the Babylonians and Assyrians, by our own great Cyrus, by the Greeks, and now by the Romans. They are a perpetual footstool for the princes of conquest to climb on. How could a great king arise out of them?"

"Listen," said he, and he read from a tattered, yellowed scroll he held in his hands. "'I see him, but not now; I behold him, but not near—a star shall come out of Jacob, and a scepter shall rise out of Israel'" (Numbers 24:17). When he finished, he added, softly but firmly: "They are the words of the prophet Balaam— and Balaam was not a Hebrew! He was a renowned seer from the valley of the Euphrates, near Carchemish. *He was from our part of the world!*"

I pondered this, carefully. When Balthasar arrived to join us, Caspar repeated his discovery. We went again onto the rooftop and deliberated long into the night as we peered up at the glowing, celestial sign. By morning we had agreed: a king was soon to be born among the lowly Hebrews, and we would journey to their distant land to seek him out and honor his coming.

We made hurried preparations for the pilgrimage, hoping that we might still arrive in time. The trip would take weeks, and require a sizable entourage and the assembling of sufficient provisions. There was also the matter of the gifts with which we would pay our tribute to the newborn king. We raided the temple treasury as well as our own personal coffers to come up with what seemed to be offerings suitable for the august occasion.

Three long months after the first sighting of the fiery jewel ascending in the East, we arrived bone weary and somewhat bedraggled at the gate of the city Jerusalem, and the excitement of anticipation beat with renewed vigor in my breast. The goal was at hand now, for Jerusalem had been the city of the Hebrew kings for centuries. It would be a simple matter to discover within the royal family the new addition destined for incomparable greatness.

Being priests ourselves, we made our way to the temple area and began asking our question: "Where is the one who has been born king of the Jews?" They responded with puzzlement on their faces. "But you surely know," we insisted. "We saw his star in its ascending, and have traveled far to venerate him." To our amazement, no one had the slightest notion of what we were talking about.

Crestfallen after that same scene was repeated over and over, we were on the verge of admitting we had erred in our interpretation of the star. But just then, one of the priests who manifested an air of authority came over to where we sat and informed us that the king, Herod, desired an audience with us. Was it merely a courtesy that he was extending to us, as foreign dignitaries? Or were we moving one step closer to our destination?

The audience was confusing, and drawn out. The king seemed not at all pleased by our visit. He appeared to be extremely agitated, asking questions, probing for information. His cold, piercing eyes seemed to burn holes through me as he inquired when the star first appeared, and where in the sky, and in what manner, and what we understood it to portend. My companions and I answered as best we could, though perplexed by his strange behavior. Should he not be pleased that his successor would achieve unprecedented heights of greatness? Should he not be thrilled that we had gone to such lengths to bow before the new king?

But no. He would leave the chamber suddenly and be gone for long periods, only to return just as suddenly and renew the questioning. When he reentered the room the final time, he looked more vexed than ever, but he invited us to sit and sup with him—and as we did so, he shared with us what he had eventually learned. At his command, one of his scribes read to us from a prophecy of which we were not aware: "And you, Bethlehem, in the land of Judah, are by no means least among the rulers of Judah; for from you shall come a ruler who is to shepherd my people Israel" (Matthew 2:6, from Micah 5:2).

Herod informed us that Bethlehem was but an hour's ride to the south, where we would need to search diligently for the child since he had not been able to ascertain further who, or where, he might be. He bid us share our discovery with him on our return, that he also might go to him in the proper spirit of adoration.

Night had fallen by the time we emerged from the king's palace. I felt a chill run through my bones, and it seemed to have nothing to do with the night air. A glance at Caspar and Balthasar told me they felt it too. Our excitement had been greatly diminished by the disturbing encounter with King Herod.

But my spirit soared within me when I looked up into the starry sky and saw again the brilliant beacon shining there. It had led us this far; we were too close to the goal to surrender hope now. Quickly we found the road south and followed it down into a fertile valley, and then up a winding route through the hills to the village at our long journey's end.

It was so late that the streets were nearly deserted. To our questions of where to find the recently born king, we were met with vacant stares. In weary desperation, we found ourselves in the courtyard of a small inn. It was full up, we learned, but the innkeeper was kind enough to invite us inside for a brief rest and a bit of refreshment. I was about to make our usual inquiry of him when a thought flashed into my mind: *We're asking the question in the wrong way!* We *know he's destined for kingship—but* they *don't!* When the innkeeper served us, I asked him simply: "Do you know of a baby having been born here in Bethlehem recently?"

He smiled, pensively. "Only of one, a boy," he said. "It happened several nights ago, right out there in one of my stables." A look of pain momentarily appeared on his countenance as he recalled the incident, but I barely noticed it, for my heart was pounding in my chest.

"Then he's right here? In your inn?"

No, he said, informing us of how he had managed to secure more suitable accommodations for them immediately afterward. We eagerly requested directions to the place, but a cloud of mistrust passed over the innkeeper's face. Only with some difficulty were we finally able to convince him that we meant the child no harm, that our purpose in coming was to pay homage to him. That surely puzzled the innkeeper, but he shared with us the last bit of information we needed to put all the pieces together.

There was no sleep for us the rest of the night. We huddled against the warmth of our camels, gazing into the sky. So many days we had waited for the curtain of night to descend so that we might keep our appointed vigil. Now we sat in holy silence waiting for the veil to lift, that we might rise with the dawn and go to him at last.

When the sun's first rays broke over the eastern mountains, we made our way through the narrow streets to the house of which we had been told. As Caspar rapped on the door, I trembled with a surge of rising doubt. Could this humble abode possibly be the correct destination of our quest? Would the babe within really be the bearer of the promise disclosed in the star? I was seized with a sudden panic, a growing sense of foolishness.

But then the door was open before us and a man was standing there with perplexity all over his rugged features. I realized immediately that he was of the laboring class, a man who earned his bread with the skill of his rough hands. Again I trembled with the realization of the audacity of our venture.

We were beginning to introduce and explain ourselves to him when a gentle voice from within the house interrupted us, a woman's voice, saying, "Let them come in, dear Joseph." Quietly he stepped aside, and we entered.

There was something disturbingly unreal about the scene. Three men of great learning and noble bearing, paying a call on a family of simple peasants. An awkward reversal of customary human roles. And yet it was the calm dignity of the young mother that put *us* at ease; she accepted readily the marvel of our having come. We gazed intently at the tiny infant nestled in her arms. Nothing remarkable about him…except the eyes. They were so alert, seemed to take in everything around him, seemed to focus so intently.

But what kind of greatness was possible from these humble beginnings? I had no answer. I, who prided myself on the depth and breadth of my worldly wisdom, had no answer. Impulsively I sank to my knees in a gesture of reverence...my companions also. The mother was quite embarrassed by our act of obeisance, but we would not be deterred—even though we couldn't grasp the why and the wherefore of it. Yielding to a wisdom far superior to our own, we could do no more than trust that our homage was somehow not misdirected, not in vain.

The parents of the child protested vigorously that they could not accept the gifts we had brought. These did seem strangely out of place—the pouch of fine gold dust; the costly and fragrant resins so important for the religious rituals attending royalty. But we prevailed upon them to accept the myrrh and gold and frankincense on the babe's behalf, as tokens of our veneration.

The journey homeward was made at a more leisurely pace once we had gotten beyond the borders of Herod's land—for our dreams had warned us not to return to him with news of the child. The star had disappeared from the sky now, but that did not disturb us. It had served its purpose—and we had served ours, of that we were inwardly sure. We could not really fathom the meaning of it. For we had set out in search of an earthly king; how could we have known the real nature of the reign he would usher in? You know. You know, so much better than I, what his kingship really consists in. And in response, you make your own journeys of adoration—for wherever you gather in the spirit of his lordship, you do him homage.

And you have learned from him the most marvelous of truths, which I in my lofty wisdom was only dimly able to perceive, and only after long and painstaking reflection: that the gift of love is of more value than all the gold in the universe, and the gift of oneself is the greatest offering any person can possibly make.

That is what his coming ultimately conveys to us—and that is why his having been in our midst is the greatest gift the world will ever enjoy.

Call Me

John

Baptizer

(Luke 3:1–18)

Call me John, son of Zechariah the priest.
You know me as the Baptizer, and so I was. But I
was more, much more. Baptizing was only one part of
my mission.

Call me Prophet, if you like. But use that title with
care. Being a prophet of God is not an honor lightly to
be assumed. I was never at ease wearing the mantle of
prophet.

If you wish to accord me the greatest of accolades,
then call me...Forerunner. John the Preparer, the One
Who Went Before—for such was my urgent task. I was
the one called forth into a world of broken humanity to
light a candle in the darkness of human hearts and

minds, and to prepare you to receive him when he comes.

Do you want to know my story? But that is not proper. *I* am not the important one. *He* is the one whose story you should seek to know.

Oh, very well. I will tell you of myself—but only so that you may see more clearly the one whose sandals I was not worthy even to untie. I have diminished as he has increased, and that is as it should be—even though he was so gracious as to look upon me with high esteem.

But remember: he is the one whose coming [*or*: suffering and triumph] you are once again preparing yourselves to honor and to receive. If my story helps you do that, then it will have served a valid purpose.

I was never one to be comfortable with the trappings of polite society—wherefore I beg your forgiveness for my rough appearance. Even at a very young age, I found the ways of the so-called civilized world distasteful.

My father, Zechariah, served as a priest in the hill country of Judea, and for two weeks of each year we traveled to Jerusalem where he officiated at the great temple. He and my mother Elizabeth were deeply pious and well versed in Torah—the Law—and I benefited greatly from their humble example. My folks held much different attitudes than those of the people who came to my father for the performance of the ritual sacrifices. Even as a boy, I was aware of the coldness of these people's hearts and the lack of real concern for anything beyond their own selfish interests. Their religious practices seemed a mockery of the God whose righteousness they proclaimed in their ceremonies. And the priests in Jerusalem—they were ever so much the worse: so worldly and pompous, so unconcerned about the deeper responsibilities required by Torah.

So I found little to attract me in the ways of people. When my parents died while I was still a youth, I left civilization behind and went to live in the wilderness area around the Dead Sea. You may regard that as foolhardy, even dangerous. I found it infinitely rewarding.

The wilderness is capable of sustaining life, if you know how to tap its secrets. I knew its many wadies of clear running water, its bubbling springs, the cool shade of its numerous caves. I was content with nourishment from locusts and wild honey, and with the austerity of a simple camel-skin robe, for I took no pleasure in the usual amenities of society.

And I preferred solitude to the bustle and the clamor of the Judean villages and towns. Choosing to be alone has its advantages. It enables you to turn inward, to consider deeply the truth about yourself—and it provides the quiet calm in which the patient voice of God can begin to be heard. I became aware of the persistent tug of God on my sleeve out there in that desolate wilderness.

But I was not completely by myself. As I grew to manhood, I spent much time also in the company of the elect known as the Essenes. You know of them because many of their writings from their library at Qumran have recently been discovered; you call these the Dead Sea Scrolls.

I was deeply attracted to the ways of my Essene friends, for they were trying to purify themselves from the defilement of disobedience to the true faith of Israel. They had gone apart from the ways of the world and created a sort of holy community, an eschatological brotherhood—for they believed that God would soon bring the Day of Judgment upon all the people, and they were preparing for the blessed order of righteousness that this would usher in. To that end, they immersed the converts to their way of life in a ritual baptism, for the cleansing of their hearts from sin and the entry into a life of moral purity. They enjoined strict obedience to Torah and the prophets of old, as they awaited together the dawn of the glorious new Day.

But thrilled as I was to see the earnestness of their life of faith, the pull of God on my heart seemed to be calling me in a different direction. It is not easy being one of God's prophets, let me tell you. You never surmount the agony of possible self-deception—for you are continually uncertain how much of the words of your message are simply the fruit of your own fertile imagination.

But I did not want to go back—mark my words! I wanted to stay there in the peace and tranquility of the wilderness, away from the turmoil and corruption wrought by human hands. The Holy One of Israel would not let me. God was relentless in pursuit of me, until at last I knew I had to give in, whatever the personal consequences.

Slowly it dawned on me that what my Essene friends were doing was not really enough. We could not simply separate ourselves from the world of human striving, focused on our own salvation. We could not retreat from a world desperately in need of someone to point it in a new direction. Somehow I felt myself in the incessant grip of a divine summons to share the message of repentance with others—with anyone and everyone who would listen, rich or poor, priest or profaner, Pharisee or tax collector.

And also there was the dim realization that someone was coming—someone who would be the personal instrument of God's impending Day of Judgment—someone who even now was already out there, somewhere, waiting, preparing.

I had a task, and the task was urgent. The way must be prepared, a path must be cleared. Isaiah's words burned in my brain: "In the wilderness prepare the way of the LORD, make straight in the desert a highway for our God. Every valley shall be lifted up, and every mountain and hill be made low; the uneven ground shall become level, and the rough places a plain. Then the glory of the LORD shall be revealed" (40:3–5a).

And so I came upon them as a wild man, moving in and out of their towns, crisscrossing the countryside, preaching to them the good news. I demanded genuine repentance of them—told them they could not wear their faith like a coat that they could put on and take off as it suited them. Their faith must blaze in them so completely that it burned away all their evil tendencies. For the judgment of the LORD was surely at hand, and the unrighteous must repent in order to be saved from God's holy wrath!

Many scoffed at me, reminding me they were descendents of Abraham and Sarah and therefore God's chosen ones. I told them none but the truly penitent would escape the consequences of the coming judgment. Those who responded to my plea, I baptized, as a mark of entrance into the community of the Last Days. However, I did not send my converts off into the wilderness. They were to return to their homes and their daily lives, the difference being that they were henceforth to practice perfect obedience to all of God's precepts—even to the point of sharing their sustenance unhesitatingly with those in need. Some, though, did remain in my constant company, as disciples, and helpers.

Then there was that other element in my teaching: *he* would come. I did not know his name, or what he would look like. I only knew that one day, soon, he would burst upon the scene and the world would be turned upside down, and my work would be over.

And then, when he did come, I did not recognize him.

Are you shocked? Don't be. You would not have recognized him either, I am sure. I believe you still have trouble recognizing him. He comes to you so often in disguise, and you do not realize it was he until it is too late.

He did not arrive with a fanfare of trumpets or in the company of angels. He was just suddenly there, in the midst of the crowd, and as I moved up and down the Jordan, preaching and baptizing, I could not help but be aware of his steady penetrating gaze, day after day, as he listened attentively to every word of my message. I inquired about him, and learned that his name was Jesus, from the village of Nazareth in Galilee, a carpenter and the son of a carpenter. He had traveled many miles to be where I was.

One day he removed his sandals and walked out into the Jordan as I was baptizing the penitent. Something stirred deep within me as I returned his unwavering look—something that told me I should not be baptizing this one at all. But he insisted that I do so.

I never saw him again after that day. There was about him something so compelling that when he left, several of my own disciples went with him. I did not try to hold them back. I yearned to go with him myself. But I did not. I continued my activity in response to the prophetic call.

Does it puzzle you, that I should not have ceased instantly? Do not fool yourselves into thinking that the instruments of God's will are so easily perceived. They do not come bearing impeccable credentials. The freedom of our faith demands that we *decide* our own response to the claims on our allegiance. God will not make that decision for us.

Thus it was that when I subsequently found myself in prison and realized my own end to be near, it was crucial for me to send word through my disciples to the Nazarene who was creating such a stir throughout the countryside: "Are you the one who is to come, or are we to wait for another?" (Matthew 11:3; Luke 7:19) His response reassured me that my work had indeed not been in vain, nor my hopes misplaced. He pointed around him to the signs of the inbreaking power of God's reign, and praised all too highly the value of my own modest contribution.

In the end, his ministry overcame my nagging bewilderment. You say you don't quite understand? But don't you see? *Jesus did not precisely fulfill MY own personal expectations of him.* Even though I was the one destined to prepare the way for his coming, *even I did not fully comprehend him.*

I had preached the impending Day of Judgment. He proclaimed the inbreaking of God's powerful reign of love.

I had emphasized the *wrath* of God that would soon be poured out upon all the unrighteous. He accented the *grace* of God that was available to all who would receive it.

I had stressed the possibility of salvation for every child of Israel who repented. He offered the gift of salvation to every child of God, without restriction.

I had insisted that the reign of God was about to overthrow once and for all the dominions of this world. Only gradually did I come to realize that the reign of God was manifesting itself already in him, in the midst of the dominions of this world. That is what I came to see at last, when he gently chided me: "Go and tell John what you have seen and heard: the blind receive their sight, the lame walk, the lepers are cleansed, the deaf hear, the dead are raised, and poor have good news brought to them. And blessed is anyone who takes no offense at me" (Luke 7:22–23). That was what he said. It was enough.

You see, at first I had wanted to receive him on my own terms, even as I was paving the way for his coming. You do not need to repeat that mistake. Now that you have listened patiently to my story, perhaps you will not be so inclined to miss him when he comes afresh into your own life this season.

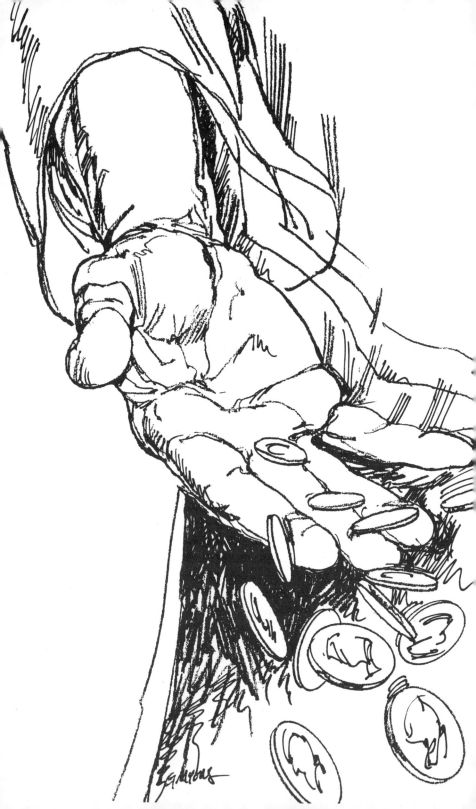

Call Me

Judas

Betrayer

*(Matthew 26:14–16, 20–25,
47–50; 27:3–5)*

Betrayer! Assassin!!
TRAITOR!!!

Ach, the epithets you have hurled at me through
the centuries. They have become synonymous with the
name itself. My name. Judas!

Would one of you name a son after me? Not likely.
And yet, Judas was once a noble—yes, an honorable—
name. How I have stained it!

My father Simon named me after one of the greatest freedom fighters our people have ever known: Judas Maccabeus, warrior priest. Many hailed him as
messiah, God's long-awaited instrument of justice and
retribution who would rise up and save his people
from the oppression that enslaved them. He led a suc-

cessful rebellion against the Syrian overlords, and cleansed the temple, which had been defiled by the hated Antiochus. But Judas was cut down in battle, and it was left to his brothers to win the war of independence he had begun. He was not the messiah, but he set in motion a century of freedom for Israel that ended only with Pompeii and the insatiable greed of the Romans.

Yes, that was my heritage. Those were the passions that inflamed my blood. Throw off the Roman dogs and usher in the Day of the Lord, the Kingdom of almighty Yahweh, our God.

That's what had attracted me to him. To Jesus, I mean. To the best friend I ever had—the friend I wound up betraying to death.

You're surprised I called him "friend"? Don't forget, he called me that, too. I was special to him. The rest of them…they were all Galileans. I was different. I was a Judean, from Kerioth.* And yet I became one of those closest to him among the ones he had chosen as his disciples. Oh, I know you always put me at the bottom of the list, because of what I did. But it wasn't that way before. I was a part of the inner circle, important enough to have been selected to serve as treasurer of the group.

I, not Matthew—the money man, ex-tax collector. I never trusted Matthew any farther than I could throw a camel. What was he doing following Jesus around? He'd already thrown in his lot with the Romans, collecting their filthy taxes for them. I never could figure out what Jesus saw in that traitor to our people.

---

* An interpretation of *Iscariot*: "the man from Kerioth," a town in southern Palestine. This is based in part on the fact that his father was similarly identified, "Simon Iscariot" (John 6:71; 13:26).

Hah! Isn't that a laugh! Me, calling Matthew a traitor. Stupid Judas! My fierce passions always did get in the way of my better judgment.

You want to know why I did it, don't you? Why I handed him over to the authorities to be killed. But I *didn't*. I mean, I delivered him up into their hands, yes. But not for the reasons you've come to imagine.

Luke and John tell you Satan entered me, forcing me to do what I did. Now there's a plea I'd love to cop. "I wasn't responsible, officer. The devil *made* me do it." It's never really that simple, let me tell you. Take it from one who's been there: the satanic forces are around us, all the time, but it's pure self-deception to blame them for our misdeeds and wrong decisions.

And I've been accused of being rapacious, greedy— of selling my friend for a few lousy silver coins. Come on, now, think! Would I have joined that ragtag band of hot-headed Galileans if all I cared about in life was making a fast buck? You didn't get rich in material things by following Jesus of Nazareth. You don't get rich betraying friendship for a little bag of blood money either. Thirty stinking pieces of silver—that's all he was worth to me? Oh, he was worth more, much more— infinitely more. The money was a ruse—to make them believe me when I said I would take them to him, to make them think that I had really changed sides.

I didn't know they would actually kill him. I never thought he would let that happen.

Oh, don't scoff at my fatal stupidity. I wasn't alone in that. Being a disciple of Jesus doesn't give you instant wisdom. Remember, those dumb fishermen weren't such hot stuff either. Did they understand, any better than I? Had they figured it out? When Jesus reinforced our growing conviction that he was indeed who we had dared to hope he was, the Messiah of God, and then told us he had to go to Jerusalem where he would suffer at the hands of the high priests and elders, big blustery Simon Peter blurted out, "No, Lord, that will never happen." So who did Jesus call Satan then, hmm? Judas of Kerioth?

And where were they when the chips were down? Why didn't they rally a force and save him, when it became apparent what was going to happen? They could have, you know. All Jerusalem was buzzing with whispered stories about the Galilean prophet who had marched right into the temple and cleansed the House of God—sort of like Judas Maccabeus had, you know? The time was ripe. Hostility toward the hated Romans was at a fever pitch. Seething resentments were bursting into the open. And on top of everything else, it was the time for the Passover celebration—the symbolic reenactment of God's deliverance of our people from the hands of the oppressor. What better time than now to make it happen all over again? And he was just the one to do it, I knew that.

I thought I knew. How easily we deceive ourselves. How easily we make our messiahs over in our own image of them.

Ach, you still want to hear my reason for betraying him. Isn't it becoming obvious to you?

I thought he wanted me to!

Remember, I joined his company of followers as a true believer. He was traveling around the Galilean countryside preaching about the Kingdom of God that was at hand, and I hungered for that to be true. I got wind of him and his message way down in Kerioth, and I set out to find him, catch up with him. Yes, I believed him, all right, perhaps believed him too fiercely. The power in him was incredible. Oh, not physical power. Quite the contrary. It was some kind of inner power, a resource the rest of us were lacking. It manifested itself in his impact on people's lives.

People were different because they had been in his presence.

But he seemed so reluctant to assume the mantle of messianic leader he was destined for. He could have had a whole army of followers; he chose but twelve. He could have announced himself openly; he preferred to be more cryptic, talking in riddles. Several times his spellbinding presence stirred a crowd to such a pitch that they tried to make him become their leader. Each time, he eluded their grasp and dashed their passionate hopes.

But now, finally, he had set his face to go to Jerusalem. That could mean only one thing: the day of reckoning was now at hand. He would openly show himself as he truly was—the one sent from God to lead us in rebellion against the Romans. His reluctance to take charge had all been part of his plan. He would not bring an army into Jerusalem; he would work from within, stir up the people to revolution *within* the city. A brilliant stroke of military genius, I thought.

They greeted him royally when he appeared. Oh, they had heard of him, all right. They were ready to follow him anywhere.

Except to a cross.

That wasn't supposed to be part of the bargain.

I was sure he was right on the verge of showing his power and declaring himself when he drove the money changers out of the temple. But then he reverted back to his old manner of behavior. He backed away from the adulation, became content once again to be merely...a teacher. Lying low. Followed by noisy crowds by day, hanging on his every word. But then slipping away, quietly, within his circle of associates, by night—confounding the authorities who couldn't reach him because of the crowds in broad daylight and couldn't find him under the cover of darkness.

But what was he waiting for? How much longer would he wait? I was puzzled.

And then it dawned on me. What if his hand were forced? What if he were put in a position where he would have no other choice but to declare himself—lay claim to his messiahship once and for all, and make the Kingdom of God come on earth by force?

Of course. It was so transparently clear. *Make* him declare that the hour had come. If he's delivered into the hands of the authorities, if he's arrested, then he'll have to come out into the open. He'll have to start using that remarkable inner power of his to topple the enemies of God from their earthly thrones and usher in the new reign he's always talking about.

And somewhere in the back of my mind, a thought was gnawing at me. Was this the way he intended for it to be? Was this, too, part of his plan? He had said that in Jerusalem he would suffer at the hands of the priests and ruling elders. But they couldn't reach him. Was it necessary for someone to help the plan succeed?

I should have consulted with him. But I didn't. There was still that nagging feeling that beneath the calm exterior he was reluctant to seize the reins of power. What if he called me off? Perhaps even slipped out of Jerusalem altogether?

So I acted on my own. I went to the chief priests and offered to sell them the information they required to get Jesus into their hands quietly.

Well, I had to give them *some* story. I couldn't exactly tell them I was doing it so he could overthrow them. I let them think I was disgruntled with his phony messianic pretensions, that he and we would all be better off if he were removed from the scene. They were so elated they paid me off, right then and there, and promised more if it went off successfully.

What exactly did I disclose to them? Where he would be, after dark, and when. And, oh yes, I agreed to identify him with a kiss, so they could be certain they arrested the right man in the dark of night.

I went back and shared one last meal with Jesus and the others. He talked about the act of betrayal, right there at the supper. I was lying right next to him, reclining on his breast. We were sharing the same dish that we dipped our crusts of bread in. When he said one of us would betray him, a chill ran through me. How did he know what I was already doing? And did he want me to go through with it or not? "The Son of Man goes as it is written of him," he said (Matthew 26:24a). He often talked that way, saying "Son of Man" when he apparently meant himself. "The Son of Man is going as it has been determined" (Luke 22:22). So I was right! He wanted it this way. It was part of the plan. But then he said, "but woe to that one by whom he is betrayed!" And I was all confused again. So I asked him, "Am I the one to do it, Master?" (Matthew 26:25, paraphrase) His answer didn't help. "So you say," was all he said.

I left the upper room in a rush, knowing I must do what I had to do—for his own good—but not being able to face his burning gaze any longer.

I led them to him, later that night—led the henchmen of the chief priests out to a garden called Gethsemane, where he had frequently gone during the week to be alone with his thoughts and his struggles and his God. The crowd with me was armed to the teeth. How stupid, I thought. You don't really need that—and it wouldn't do you any good if he chose to oppose you.

He called me "friend" again, as I placed the identifying kiss on his cheek. Then he asked me what I was about. Didn't he know? Didn't he!?

Turmoil ensued, as they took him in hand, forcefully. I slipped away under cover of darkness—waiting for what I knew now would surely take place. Once he was in their hands, the climactic movement in the messianic drama would necessarily begin. Now that his hand had been forced, he would declare openly before the Sanhedrin that he truly was the one sent from God to lead God's people into the dawning kingdom of righteousness and freedom. And the Sanhedrin and the masses would flock to his side and follow his leadership in the overthrow of God's enemies and ours.

But that isn't what happened. You know that. So do I...now.

You know—I know, now—how fatally stupid I was. You know—I know, now—that his kingdom wasn't that *kind* of kingdom at all. He didn't do anything by force—that's what his kingdom was all about.

And when finally I realized that he wasn't going to resist, that the power at work within him wasn't that kind of power, it was too late. They had decided to kill him.

I went back to the priestly high command. "This wasn't supposed to happen!" I said. "Too bad," said they. "Take back your money!" I cried.

It was too late for that. It didn't matter now. Do you wonder that I couldn't live with myself any longer? Realizing in the end the horror of what I had set in motion, the fatal stupidity of my misunderstanding?

If you learn anything from my story, learn this: don't make me into a scapegoat. Betrayal is so easy. You don't have to have very vicious motives to do it. Don't make the mistake of assuming that because once upon a time one man betrayed him, all the betrayals are over with. We each have the capacity to be a Judas of Kerioth.

And beware of this—oh, especially beware of this: beware of making him over into your own image, as I did. Beware of acting foolishly out of what you *want* him to be, instead of what he offers himself to you to be.

I have but one final thought to share with you. I understand that one of his last words as he hung on that cross, dying, was a word of forgiveness. "Father, forgive them; for they do not know what they are doing" (Luke 23:34).

I didn't know what I was doing. Did he forgive even me?

Did he?

Call Me
Pilate
Governor

(Matthew 27:11–26)

Truth. He wanted to talk about "truth" to me. I've come into the world for the purpose of telling people the truth, he said. Hah! "What *is* truth?" I asked him (John 18:37-38).

Not that I was all that interested in what he might answer. I knew what truth is from my vantage point. Power. Power is truth. That's what I showed him. I, Pontius Pilate, Procurator of the Roman province of Judea, servant of my lord the Emperor Tiberius, showed him.

You're surprised that I'm dressed like this? But isn't this the way government officials are supposed to look in your day? Button-down collar, three-piece vested. Conservative cut, but just the right splash of color.

I am Pontius Pilate, appointed head of a conquered people, obedient to the state I serve faithfully, subservient to its causes, its precepts. I'm easier to recognize like this. You don't understand? You will. Ah, but you will.

Yes, I'm the one who sentenced your leader to be executed. I don't deny it. I'm not exactly proud of it, but it was a job to be done. I washed my hands of the whole affair a long time ago. I had my orders, you know. "Keep the peace." Maintain law and order. Use whatever force is necessary to keep matters from getting out of hand. So I did. I was just doing my job. Do you really think you would have handed down a different verdict, if you had been in my place?

I'd had my eye on your Jesus of Nazareth for some time. Does that surprise you? Listen, you don't get to be governor of a Roman province by being indifferent to potential troublemakers. I had my hands full of insurrections and murderous rebels and disturbances of the peace from the moment I stepped off the galley. Let me tell you, the ones who give vent to violence are the easy ones to control. Like that fool Barabbas. Caught him in the act. The ones who use words are harder to get a handle on. I remember one in particular that Herod, up north in the Galilean province, had to deal with. Fellow named John. They called him "Baptist." He used words to stir up the people. Herod disposed of him.

This Jesus seemed to me a whole lot more dangerous than the rebel Barabbas. Reports from my spies told me he was giving the people new ideas and they were following him around like puppy dogs. Believe you me, there's nothing more threatening to entrenched power than people with an idea. You've got to stamp it out, before the spark ignites and becomes a raging inferno of new ideas and alternative possibilities. Power fears people thinking for themselves. Yes, this Jesus bore watching. His influence could be very unsettling.

He was no real threat so long as he stayed out there in the boondocks, in and out of Capernaum, up and down the Jordan River valley. Anyway, he was in Herod's domain then. But I figured he'd come here sooner or later—come to Jerusalem, center of his people's religion and political life for centuries. Sure enough, he finally did.

I was getting regular reports on him from my staff, from the moment he entered the city. His arrival caused an uneasy stir among my soldiers. It seemed like the whole city had gone out to greet him that day. The whole garrison was on edge, and on constant alert. One word, one signal from him and we would have had a monumental uprising on our hands.

I was sure that was precisely what we were facing when word reached me that he had provoked a bitter confrontation in the outer hall of the temple. But the chaos there did not spill over into the streets, and he adopted a quieter profile after that. My staff reports informed me that he had taken up the mantle of teacher again, sharing his message with huge crowds by day, slipping away quietly by night. Don't be deceived, I reminded them. He's all the more dangerous for that.

But frankly, I was surprised when I was awakened at daybreak that particular morning with the news that his own religious leaders had arrested him and were wanting to dump him on my doorstep. They weren't anybody's fools, I thought to myself as I was getting dressed. They recognized the threatening power of a new idea too.

"On what charge is he being brought before me?" I asked. On the charge of disloyalty to the Roman state, I was told. He keeps preaching about a new kingdom.

He's set himself up to be the king of the Jews. "Oh? And is he?" I asked. "We have no king but Caesar," they protested in reply.

Smart fellows. They knew on which side their bread was buttered. They understood the value of political expediency.

He was different from any other person who ever stood before me accused of so major a crime—I'll grant you that. He wasn't cowed by my high office, or position of authority, or the trappings of governmental pomp. He didn't plead innocence or beg for mercy. I resented that. I doubt that I would have ordered him to be scourged were it not for that...that piercing gaze of his, and that damnable insolent self-control. *He didn't knuckle under!* How dare he!

He presumed to face me as an equal. By Jupiter, it was even worse than that. His bearing seemed to call into question my very authority over him. I reminded him of the sorry predicament he was in. "It's in my hands to have you crucified or set you free," I said to him. He answered that I had no more authority over him than what his god allowed me to have. The nerve of him! (John 19:10–11).

Did I consider him guilty of anything? Of course I did. Oh, I know your writers tell a somewhat different story. They suggest I found him innocent but sentenced him to be killed anyway. Now what kind of administration of Roman justice is that, I ask you? I may have been buried out in that backwater province about as distant from the center of power in Rome as you could get, but I was a Roman provincial governor all the same. I had a duty and I performed it. I sentenced to death a man who, if he had had his way, would have toppled the very foundations of the Roman Empire with nothing more powerful than words. Ideas. Truth! Hah! His kind of truth is very dangerous indeed. I knew as he stood calmly before me that there could be no half measures with this man. Either you joined up with him or you opposed him with all your might. Around him, you gave up any pretext to neutrality.

His own people had stirred up a mob against him, right outside the palace. They were crying for his blood. I wondered how many of them had been hailing him as King David's heir only a few days before. Mobs are simple to deal with because everyone temporarily surrenders the luxury of informed judgment. You only have to manipulate the handful of leaders who are manipulating the mindless masses. I went out and offered to hand over a prisoner to them. As a gesture of my good will. As a way of keeping them in my pocket.

They screamed for Barabbas.

Barabbas, the rebel, the freedom fighter. Barabbas who would topple the Roman government with a sword. Barabbas who would fight to establish justice by unjust means. So I let them have Barabbas.

You think I was daft? Oh, how little you understand the workings of the official mind. I knew exactly what I was doing. Give them their Barabbas. He'd be back in prison soon enough. Jesus from Nazareth was by far the more dangerous of the two. He rejected political accommodation. He opposed the twin principles of compromise and expediency. He challenged the power of military might and the authority of the state to expect unblinking obedience from its citizens. He intended to set people free by arming them with nothing more than *truth*. I tell you, there is nothing half so revolutionary as that!

Barabbas and his kind I could deal with. They play the game by the same rules I and Caesar do. They merely want to exchange one set of rulers for another. Jesus threatened to undermine the whole system, tried to introduce an entirely new approach to human affairs and human struggles and human conflict. With forgiveness and mercy, instead of justice. With love instead of force, influence instead of manipulation. Moral principle instead of political expediency and business efficiency. Boundless compassion instead of the pursuit of self-interest. You don't stay in power long if you let those kinds of ideas flourish unopposed.

Yes, I gave them their Barabbas all right—and sentenced Jesus to be executed immediately.

So now you despise me for having had the audacity to condemn your leader to death by crucifixion. Are you sure of that?

Don't you see? I did you a favor by getting him out of your hair, so you could go back to business as usual even as you parade around with his name on your lips.

Face it—you don't like his truth any more than I did. When the chips are down, you fall back on the same policies I live by. You have no king but Caesar either. Do you?

Item: Our leaders knew how to keep the people contented and conveniently distracted. Offer them bread and circuses. A steady stream of amusements to occupy their attention and dull their senses. What about you? You American Christians say he's your Lord, but you Christians spend more money on athletic events and rock concerts and dog food than you provide in support of his cause. Hah! He knew what you *needed*. But we know something better, don't we? We know what you *want*! We offer it. You take it.

Item: Our leaders said, "Be obedient to Caesar, first, last, and always." He told you to distinguish between what was Caesar's due and what was your god's. We said, "Sacrifice your principles when the national self-interest demands it." He told you God and not the state is to be the lord of your judgments. But you go right on pleading patriotism at the expense of human need just like I did, giving succor to tyrants and demagogues around the world because it's in the interest of "national security."

Ah yes, now you're beginning to see me as I am. Now you're beginning to recognize Pontius Pilate, Caesar's faithful servant, aren't you?

Item: You despise me because I handed down the verdict that caused him to be nailed onto a cross where he hung until death. Oh, I know crucifixions aren't a very pretty way to be executed. They weren't intended to be. They were supposed to function as a deterrent against capital crimes. It didn't work out that way, but we kept on doing it—and so do you! You have Christian governors giving the go-ahead to hammer the nails into contemporary crosses all around you. Do you lift a finger in protest?

Item: I represent the propitious exercise of worldly power. He denied my authority so I used the power at my disposal to have him killed. In my world, bullets and bombs and crosses are still more powerful than ideas. Is it so different in your world? Who won, in the end? He, or I? You be the judge. Your actions, your allegiances, your commitment, already are the judge. Face it—I won, and you know it. When your backs are against the wall, you play the game by the same rules I do. Bomb them into submission. Oppose force with greater force. You're not against the kind of power I exemplified. *You rely on it!*

There is a rumor circulating that he didn't stay dead. His followers spread the word that *he* won after all, that his god conquered the worst that my worldly power could do to him, ending my dominion once and for all. Well, I don't know about that. I know that I released his body for burial to one of the members of the Sanhedrin, who was secretly a follower of him. I know that a short time later the tomb in which his body was placed was discovered to be empty. I don't put much stock in that. After all, it doesn't prove anything one way or the other.

There's only one way you're going to convince me that he was victorious in the end. If I should see *him* in *you*—then I'll know he really got the best of me. Not until then will I give any credence to the rumors of his so-called resurrection.

So who won? He? Or I? You be the judge. Your life...*is*...the judge!

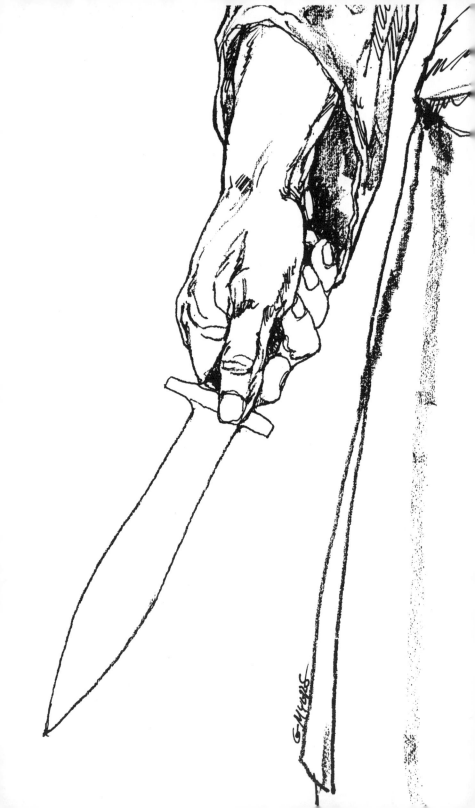

Call Me
Barabbas
Rebel

(Mark 15:6–15)

They killed him instead of me. It should have been me they nailed up there on that cross. He took my place. He died for me.

I didn't ask him to do it. I don't ask no one no favors. Not me, not Barabbas.

So why did he do it? Why did he go and let them crucify him? He didn't have to. He coulda gotten off with just a warning, maybe a few lashes. He coulda hightailed it out of the city and left the rough stuff to us what is used to it. He had no cause, goin' off and gittin' himself killed like that.

Jesus, why did you have to go and die in my place? Why couldn't you just leave me alone to face my fate?

Now I can't shake free of you and your strange ways, as long as I live.

I shoulda known. Simon had told me. Oh yeah, he'd really done a number on Simon. Turned him right around in his tracks.

Simon was one of us, one of mine. You call him Simon the Zealot. That's what we were, all right— zealots. Freedom fighters, zealous for the right, unswerving in our opposition to the Roman oppressors. My people had drunk from the bitter dregs of tyranny and we had said, "Enough!" No more!

We were zealous for the righteous wrath of our God Yahweh to be poured out mercilessly on those who enslaved us—and we were willing to the death to be instruments of that wrath. We struggled in secret against the villainous authority of Rome and all who supported it. We knew the day would come when we would be strong enough to rise up openly and throw off the shackles of oppression in a violent and bloody revolution. In the meantime, we started little brush-fires, nipped at the flanks. The assassination of a Roman sympathizer here, a robbery there. Stirring up a riot now and then to keep the Roman army off balance.

But Simon kept telling me I oughta check out this Nazarene he was following around. I said, "Simon, that's what we sent *you* to do. You were supposed to get a line on him and report back to us. Let us know what his plans are, how much of a following he has, when and where he's likely to strike."

That wasn't what Simon reported back. Simon tried to convince us that this Jesus of Nazareth was no less than the real thing. A Messiah with a difference. "He thinks you can only change the world by changing the people in it. One by one. He says we've got to start loving each other, even our enemies," Simon said. I said, "Simon, that's garbage. What kind of revolutionary spouts nonsense like that? And why haven't you slit the throat of that tax collector yet, the one that's been befriended by your Jesus—what's his name—Matthew?"

But Simon just shook his head at what he considered my dumb confusion and said, "Barabbas, you've got to come with me and meet him. Listen to him. Find out for yourself what kind of impact he has on people." I said, "Thanks but no thanks. I've got my own work to do. And look," I said, "you can't just keep turning the other cheek when the bullies of this world knock you down. Sooner or later you're gonna run out of places for them to strike you. No, you gotta pick yourself up out of the dirt and fight back. Show them you're as tough as they are, so they'll go away and leave you alone."

Simon wouldn't listen to me. He was listening to a different voice than mine now. He went his way, I went mine—he to follow his gentle Jesus, I to incite a bloody riot in Jerusalem right before the Passover and get caught and get tossed in the slammer.

My "trial" was quick and to the point. That Pilate, he don't beat around the bush. His soldiers announced the charges against me, and the guv'ner sat there coldly staring at my dirty rags. "Guilty," he said, with all the emotion of a man flicking a dead fly off his mantle. "Take him out and crucify him. Let him be a lesson to the others."

I had expected it. I had known it would come to that, sooner or later. I was ready to die. In this dog-eat-dog world it's kill or be killed. In my case it was both. The flames of the revolution are fueled by the blood of its martyrs. Someone else would pick up where I left off. Resistance to oppression isn't eliminated so easily.

Still, I spent a restless night. When suddenly you're condemned to die, life takes on a different appearance. It smacks you in the face with jarring intensity. Every second becomes precious. You gulp huge mouthfuls of life like a drowning man gasping for air. You drink life in through all your senses. Sounds you never heard, smells you never noticed, now flood over you and you savor each one, strain to seize it, make it linger in your brain—try to stop the flow of time, hold onto the moment—to no avail.

They would come for me at sunrise. Make me shoulder the weight of the crosspiece, the instrument of my own death, as they marched me to the killing ground. Drive jagged metal spikes into my wrists. Ram the cross into a hole in the ground and leave me hanging there in agony, laughing at me as life slowly and painfully slipped away.

You don't want to think about it, but you have to, to prepare yourself for it.

Sunrise came. The soldiers didn't.

An hour, then another, dragged by like an eternity. The waiting, the wondering, the jarring uncertainty.

Then, footsteps, coming closer. A key in the latch, the heavy door being swung open.

There were only two of them, standing there. Not enough to escort a man to his execution. What then? More pain, more humiliation? I knew the tortures the Roman soldiers liked to dish out on condemned criminals, for the sport of it. Had they come to amuse themselves at my expense?

"Get out, scum!" said the taller one of the two. "Pilate says you're to go free. Lucky dog."

I stared in astonishment.

He answered my silent question. "The Governor decided to crucify somebody else in your place, and appease the crowd by setting you free. Go on, get out of here. And don't let us see you in Jerusalem or your pardon will be short-lived."

"Wh-who?" I mumbled as I stumbled through the open doorway. "Who got it instead of me?"

"I dunno," he said, "some fanatic or other, from up in Galilee. Jesus, I think his name was. Now beat it."

Jesus, his name was. Jesus. My name.

You didn't know that? Ironic, isn't it? Jesus Barjoseph, called Messiah, called Son of God, was crucified instead of Jesus Barabbas, rebel. Barabbas. That means "son of the father." Figure that one out.

He took my place, on the cross.

Of all the people in the world he coulda died in place of, he had to go and die in place of me. Him and his ways of peace and love and going the second mile—and he...walked...*my* last mile. With *my* cross tearing into his raw flesh.

Why couldn't he have picked a more worthy man to stand in for? Why didn't he slip quietly out of Jerusalem after my men and I started the riot and increased the tension among the Roman authorities tenfold? Oh God, *why me*?

You think it's easy, living with the memory of that? You think I got a lucky reprieve, that I got off scot-free and could live out the rest of my life in peace and tranquility? Hah! Fat lot you know! Every day I live, every breath I take, I have to come face to face with the fact that he died so I could live. He'd said we were supposed to love our enemies instead of hating them and striving for their destruction. I and my ways were surely his enemy. He had loved me...to death.

Change the world...by changing people. And change people...by loving them...no matter what.

I'm confused. I don't have it figured out. I wrestle with it night and day. That's why I'm sharing it with you. Maybe you can figure it out.

He said, "The greatest love you can have for somebody is when you give up your life on their behalf."

I dunno.

You figure it out.

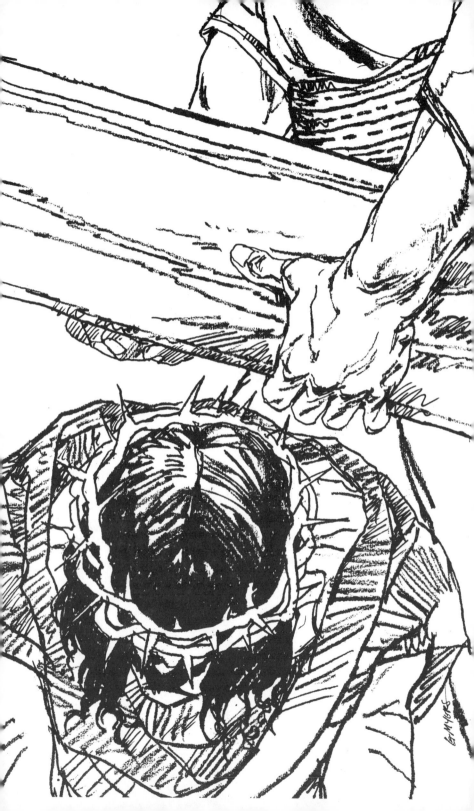

Call Me

Simon

of Cyrene

(Mark 15:12–26)

I did not want to do it. I did not volunteer, you understand. Years later, I came to rejoice at the honor of that burden. But at the time, there was no honor in carrying the cross of a man condemned to die. There was only the ache and the anguish—and a burning hatred toward those despicable Romans who were executing another of my people on one charge or another.

You know of me as Simon of Cyrene, the man who literally bore the cross of the Christ. You know little else about me. If I share my story with you, it is only so that you may see reflected in my life the impact of the one whose cross *both* you and I are called to bear.

I come from the large Jewish settlement in the city of Cyrene, on the Mediterranean coast of Libya in north-

ern Africa. You will remember that we Jews had become scattered throughout the entire Near East from
the time of the Exile onward. But we continued to
retain a gnawing hunger for the homeland of our ancestors, no matter where we lived, no matter how many
generations we had been away.

So you can well appreciate why I would have chosen to migrate with my family to Palestine, to settle in
one of the numerous villages of Judea and sharpen
further my skills as a craftsman. My work in bronze
and copper came to be in much demand among the
more well-off of my people, so that we were able to
make a go of things. And we would have done even
better than that, were it not for the oppressive taxes
that the Roman dogs exacted from everything I was
able to sell.

Busy as I was, I had found it possible to close up
my shop for several weeks to journey with my family
to the holy city of Jerusalem for the annual celebration
of the Passover. This is the most special of all our
religious observances, recalling God's leading of our
people out of slavery into freedom and the promised
land, and there is no more desirable place to observe it
than in Jerusalem. Zion. The City of David.

We had managed to secure lodgings and a room
for the Passover meal. With other of my kinsmen, I
had gone up to the magnificent temple restored by
King Herod to buy and sacrifice the paschal lamb.
That evening we had met together for the solemn Feast
of Unleavened Bread. It was a tremendously moving
experience for me, a Jew from faraway Cyrene, to be
here in the Holy City for this most memorable of nights.
How could I have known then of another meal being
shared in Jerusalem that very hour—and of the events
just beginning to unfold, in which I would soon find
myself caught up so unexpectedly?

The night was long, and full of much conviviality once the ritual itself had ended. Sleep was unthinkable. We talked on and on, sharing our memories and our hopes, till dawn began to break on the horizon. I left my wife and young sons at our rented quarters and went out into the city to walk in the brisk morning air.

Jerusalem was jammed with people, even in the early morning. Tens of thousands of pilgrims had streamed in for the Passover feast. Some were asleep in open doorways. A steady drone floated in the air, the buzz of a thousand conversations.

The Romans were uneasy. Jerusalem was always a powder keg. Jerusalem at Passover was nothing short of terrifying for the garrison of imperial soldiers. There were simply too many people around, too many potential threats to the keeping of a very fragile peace. The slightest spark could ignite a raging conflagration.

We were always chafing at the Roman rule, even in the calmest of times. But the latest procurator, a man named Pilate, had had the audacity to raid the temple treasury to pay for the building of a new aqueduct. With the surging undercurrent of unrest, the Romans had cause to be nervous. It seemed that hardly a month went by without yet another messianic pretender trying to stir up the populace and lead them in revolt. The Romans had their hands full putting down one rebellion after another. Even the slightest whisper of a possible messiah was an occasion for arrests and scourgings and dire warnings.

So it was, that fateful morning, that the crowds were buzzing with talk of yet another arrest. No one seemed to know much about him, except for the rumors that he was from the north country, Galilee. None of us really expected we would hear any more of the matter, certainly not at the height of the Passover. And then it all happened with such a burst of suddenness.

The sound of trampling feet, drawing closer. The rough voices of Roman soldiers, ordering the street to be made clear. Occasional high wails of women, grieving.

And then I saw him.

He was bent low under the weight of a large beam, dragging it along step by painful step. Blood was matted in his hair and ran down his face, from plaited thorn branches pressed down onto his head. Knowing the Romans all too well, I was sure that beneath his robe his back must be raw from the whip. It seemed to me for a moment that the weight of the whole world was crushing down on his shoulders.

He fell to one knee. No one moved to help him. A soldier ordered him to get up, to get moving again. Finally, slowly, he struggled back onto his feet, staggered a few more agonizing steps—then fell again.

He was only a few feet from me. I inched forward for a moment, for I was transfixed by the look of his haunting eyes. It was as though, in the midst of that pain-racked face, there was a sense of peace. I was spellbound by those eyes.

That's why I didn't notice what was happening around me until it was too late. The way the rest of the crowd had pulled back, in fear. The sudden shock of a hand seizing me by the shoulder. And a rough Roman voice in my ear: "He's too weak, Jew. *You* carry it for him. After all, he's *your* king, isn't he?" And then he laughed—a harsh, coarse laughter.

I was petrified by the order. But I had little choice in the matter. And then he started to get up again, actually took another halfstep forward. That's when I rushed forward, as much in pity as in response to the command, and lifted the crosspiece from his back. He looked at me—looked right into me, it seemed. And those blazing eyes of his spoke a silent "thank you."

The procession moved on through the streets—now with me as a reluctant part of it. I followed him, kept pace with his weary footsteps, the sight of his bruised body causing me to forget the weight on my back and the pain seeping into my muscles. Onward we trudged, through one of the city gates and on out to a rocky hill shaped strangely like a skull.

I laid down my load and watched, exhausted, as they fastened it to an even longer, heavier beam, forming a cross. They stripped off his robe and stretched him out upon it....Nailed him to it.

I slipped unnoticed into the crowd of onlookers as they were raising the cross erect and jamming it into a hole they had prepared for it. I was fearful for my own life, for I had caught a fleeting glimpse of two other crosses being lashed together and had no idea who they were intended for. Shuddering in my aching weariness, I looked from a distance at the man hanging there on the center cross, the man sentenced to die a cruel death by crucifixion—the man whose cross I had carried. And I thought to myself: I do not know the crime he has been condemned for. *I do not even know his name.*

Not then, I didn't, though I learned it quickly enough. As I stumbled half-blindly back to the rented room, the city was all abuzz with the news that a certain Jesus, from Nazareth, had been crucified that very morning. "Why?" I asked. "What was he guilty of?" Of being a threat to the authorities, I was told. "Another of God's messiahs," they said. "See what it got him for his troubles."

And then I remembered what the soldier had said to me—remembered also what had been attached to the top of the cross: *king.* Your king. King of the Jews.

How strange, I thought. He hadn't looked anything at all like a king. Still less like the leader of an uprising.

I told my family all that had happened that morning and made haste to flee Jerusalem before nightfall, before the beginning of the Sabbath. I did not know but that they might be arresting others—his followers, and anyone who had had anything to do with him. What had begun as a pilgrimage of holy joy had ended on a note of shame and the threat of disaster.

Only gradually did I come to realize that that day of infamy had been a beginning and not an ending. Tales filtered into our village as the months turned into years—tales of a spellbinding prophet from up north, from Galilee, who had been crucified in Jerusalem during a celebration of the Passover. It was chilling when I heard them speak of him that way. It was even more chilling when they whispered cautiously another tale: that this man's followers were convinced that he had appeared to them newly and strangely alive—that God had actually raised him up from death. They were spreading the word that this crucified Jesus was really and truly the Messiah of God after all.

I could not put the stories out of my mind, ridiculous as they seemed. And especially I could not ignore the stories that were circulating about what he had said and taught. He had said that God is like a merciful and loving Father who is willing to forgive our failures to be righteous in the Law. He had taught that we should be able to leave the Law behind, to go beyond it, in being loving and forgiving just as God is. He had said that we should even love our enemies, and do good to those who persecute us.

I was stunned as I heard these things. How could I ever forget that look of incredible peacefulness on his bleeding face? How could I ever forget the total absence of hatred for his persecutors from that anguished countenance? I had been bewildered at the time. I thought him perhaps dazed by the pain, possibly drugged. But now I realized. Love your enemies, he had taught. And he had loved his, even while they were killing him.

My sons were on the threshold of young manhood when I finally returned again to Jerusalem. I let them come along. It was no Passover pilgrimage this time. There was a different reason for the journey.

I had determined to seek out the community of his followers, to meet them and talk with them directly. The panic that had gripped me on the cruel day was long a thing of the past. I had to know, had to find out...about the man whose cross I had been made to bear.

Locating them was not hard. A few judicious inquiries and I found myself being led with my sons to a large house where a number of people were gathered, talking excitedly in small groups. The leader turned out to be a man with the same name as my own—except he preferred being called Peter. I told him why we had come, told him who I was. And when I spoke the words that identified the nature of my one and only contact with their Master, a dizzying hush fell over the entire room. I turned to see that they were all looking at me in astonishment. I trembled. Then the craggy-faced Simon Peter broke the silence.

"We had heard about you," he said. "But we had no idea who you were. We were certain we would never get to meet you. We were not there that day, you see. We were hiding, scared for our very lives. Only later did we discover the strength to bear up under the weight of our Messiah's cross. You, a stranger, ministered to him. You are already in his kingdom, without even realizing it."

Then he embraced me, and the whole room was full of voices and embracing and a chaos of goodwill.

And all the stories I had been hearing came to life right before my eyes.

There is so much more that could be told, but it would take too long. Of how my entire family and I joined this fledgling group of devotees, and spread the word to any who would listen. Of how, in our old age, my wife became like a mother to that worthy apostle Paul whenever he visited Jerusalem. Of how my two fine sons, Rufus and Alexander, eventually traveled with their mother all the way to Rome itself in the spreading of the message—where Rufus became one of the leaders in the young church there (Romans 16:13).

But that would only distract you from the point of my story. *He* is the point, not I. My humble contribution was merely that I happened to bear the burden of his cross for less than a single mile—and not even by choice, at that. You have the same opportunity as I—but only if you choose to. Pick up the cross of healing hurts or mending animosities or opposing injustice. Bear the cross of loving the stranger in your midst or uniting with the dreams of the oppressed or overcoming alienation wherever you find it.

Is any of that really too much to ask on behalf of someone who carried on his shoulders the burdens of all humanity?

Call Me

Senecus

Centurion

(Mark 15:22–39)

I am not the man I was. I am changed.

But God help me, I was the one who presided at his execution and nothing that happens can ever let me escape from the memory of that awful deed.

You may address me as Senecus. I am a centurion in the Second Italian Cohort of the Imperial Army of Rome. But I am also one of you. Does that astonish you? Perhaps if you will listen to my shameful story, you will come to understand…and, possibly, even to forgive.

I will not try to defend what I did, nor try to make my part in the ugly affair seem less odious than it was. For I am guilty. Ha! What a hideous irony! *He* was the innocent one I executed, and *I* was the guilty one.

Of course I didn't realize that at the time....No! That's not true. I promised you I'd play no games with truth. I cannot hide behind the disguise of ignorance. I was sure of his innocence of wrongdoing, even then— had every reason to believe his execution was not justified. Still I carried out the order.

There. You see? That was my defense—I was only obeying an order, like any good army officer should. I was simply doing my job. Even when the job was supervising a crucifixion. I blindly followed an order, even though I felt strongly that *this* order was horribly unjust. That was my crime.

It took me a long, long time before I could let him remove the weight of it from my shoulders.

I had not requested to be sent to Judea. I had not sought promotion to the rank of centurion. But neither did I refuse it when the opportunity was thrust upon me, and duty in this seething frontier backwater was the consequence. There were a thousand places I would as soon have served my emperor as dismal Jerusalem.

But we who are centurions are not so high in positions of influence as to be able to pick and choose our destiny. We rise up from the ranks, but we cannot rise very far; our lack of social and economic status prevents that. Never the glory of the horse soldier for us— the equestrian order requires money, class standing. We are the fodder, the foot soldiers. The most we can aspire to is the commission of centurion, supervision over a hundred fighting men.

That had been my fate. Showing bravery and loyalty and good judgment in battle, I had been elevated to a centurion's command, and put in charge of a company that all too soon found itself quartered in the capital of a tiny Roman province on the eastern edge of the Great Sea. And answerable to a brutal, corrupt procurator named Pontius Pilate.

Let me tell you about this Pilate. He didn't last very long as a provincial governor, you know. A few more years of bungling in Judea and he was removed from the post, and summarily dropped out of sight. It didn't come any too soon, that's for sure. He had been sent to this desolate place as one last chance to make a good showing of himself as an administrator and keeper of the Roman peace. He botched it.

He was always doing things to provoke the people into angry and sometimes violent reaction. Even though the image of Emperor Tiberius was regarded as an idolatrous abomination to their strict religious faith, he ordered us to sneak the hated standards into the city under cover of darkness and then unveil them the next day. The reaction was so intense that I was sure we would have open rebellion on our hands, till Pilate relented and had them removed. On yet another occasion, though, he sent troops out to mingle in disguise among a throng of protesting Jews. Upon receiving the signal, they drew clubs from their robes and attacked the crowd so violently that many were killed.

I thought his actions odd, but then, who was I to pass judgment on a procurator? Centurions are not supposed to think too much on our own. We are supposed to do as we are told. Questioning the decision of a superior would be insubordinate suicide.

Not that I was opposed to the proper use of force and violence. I am a soldier, remember. I have known my share of fighting, killing. And I have witnessed and presided over numerous crucifixions carried out against convicted enemies of the Roman state. *His* was not my first. Nor my last. But his was different.

There was something so utterly unjust about the whole affair from first to last. This time, instead of remaining resolute in the face of protest, the procurator passed conflicting sentences, arbitrarily and impulsively, simply to appease the populace.

I first became aware that something was going on when the barracks began to stir late in the night with word of the arrest of a man we had been keeping an eye on as a potential troublemaker. He was not a Judean. He was from Galilee. But he seemed to have gathered a fairly large following, and he had caused quite a ruckus a few days earlier in a violent confrontation with the Jewish priests in their sacred temple. But then he had adopted a low profile after that, and I had almost forgotten about him. Till news came of his arrest.

I had my own first glimpse of him early that next morning—that fateful morning. I had been ordered to Pilate's court to take charge of a prisoner being handed over by the guards of the Jewish Sanhedrin. He had his back to me when I first saw him. His hands were bound, but he did not seem to look all that dangerous. There was a sort of quiet dignity about him, in spite of his awkward predicament. Pilate kept demanding of him whether he pretended to be a king among the Jews, and the Jewish leaders in the room were hurling vicious accusations at him—about blasphemy against their God, and treason against Rome. Yet he seemed strangely unmoved by it all. I had seen prisoners standing in the presence of Roman authority many times, facing far less serious charges than these, and they either cringed in fear or lashed back in hostile belligerence. But he did neither. He remained disturbingly calm, as though it were not really he who was on trial at all.

I heard Pilate protesting to the assembled Jewish leaders that he could find no cause for any conviction of the man. But when they vehemently protested that judgment, he immediately reversed himself. He turned to me and ordered me to have the man scourged, and then to let him go (Luke 23:16).

That stunned me for a moment. A man is not scourged who is found innocent of any crime. In fact, the punishment is so severe that we call it the "halfway death." Forty brutal lashes with a barbed leather whip. Even battle-hardened soldiers sometimes shuddered at the sight.

I supervised the scourging. The strange Galilean received the blows with only a faint moan escaping from his lips, but he mercifully lapsed into unconsciousness before long. We revived him with a bucket of water when it was over.

My men then proceeded to make sport with the badly battered prisoner, as often they did when a victim of Roman justice fell into their hands. When you live in a climate of violence, you quickly become very insensitive to matters of human decency. One of them brought over a branch from a thorn tree and wound it into the shape of a wreath and forced it down upon his bleeding brow like a mock crown. Another threw an old purple robe around his shoulders and shoved a reed into his hand. Then they ridiculed him, bowing down with exaggerated mockery to hail him as "King of the Jews." Then they took the reed and struck him in the face with it, and spat on him. Finally I interrupted their cruel farce and led him back to the court of Pilate to be released and sent on his way, in agony and humiliation.*

But it was not to be. A large crowd had gathered in the square, and when Pilate had the bruised and broken body of this Jesus led out before them, the air was suddenly filled with cries for his crucifixion. My procurator was obviously dismayed. He tried to strike a bargain with the crowd, and offered to hand over to

---

* This reconstruction follows the sequence in John 19:1ff., which is somewhat different from the other three Gospels.

freedom either the man Jesus or another prisoner named Barabbas. That really astonished me, since Pilate had not found the Galilean guilty of anything, whereas Barabbas was a small-time revolutionary guilty of treason and murder. And to Pilate's surprise, the crowd yelled back, "Give us Barabbas!" Why should he have been surprised? After all, the anti-Roman rebel was a hero to them!

So finally he gave in to all the pressure, and made his second arbitrary decision of the day: he ordered me to have Barabbas released from prison—and to take Jesus out and have him crucified, like the crowd demanded.

I was troubled inside. The scourging had been enough, I thought. And scourging was never administered in addition to further punishment. The double sentence was beyond the bounds of Roman justice. But I did as I was told. My only consoling thought was that the effect of the beating would serve to shorten his agony of slow death on the cross.

There were two others, already convicted, who were waiting in prison for their sentence of crucifixion to be carried out. I had them brought out as well. When all the arrangements had been made, a long heavy beam was laid across each one's shoulders and the grisly procession of soldiers and condemned men began its slow journey through the Jerusalem streets.

I felt uneasy about the one, the Galilean. I avoided his eyes—which was easy to do since his head was bent low by the weight of the cross and the agony of the scourging. Nobody had removed the crown of thorns. I started to, then thought better of it. Showing sympathy for someone condemned to die was foolhardy, even dangerous. But when he staggered under the load of the crosspiece and fell to the pavement, I took the matter into my own hands. I grabbed one of the bystanders and ordered him to carry the cross instead.

The men under my command made quick work of it once we reached the rocky hill where the executions would take place. There was quite a crowd assembled, curious, excited, eager to view the gruesome spectacle of men dying. I felt angry at them. For me, it was a job. For them, it was perverse entertainment. I wondered to myself how they would feel if it were *them* up there on a cross, instead of him.

The sound of nails being pounded into wrists and feet still haunts me in my sleep. I stationed soldiers to stand guard at the foot of each of the crosses and sat down to await the inevitable. It was only when I heard sounds like mumbled words coming from his lips that I screwed up my courage enough to peer up at him, to look into the face I had been so studiously avoiding. To my dismay, his piercing eyes seemed to be staring right at mine, and I felt a cold chill run through my bones. Then the lips moved and I heard him speak and it was as if he were speaking right at me. "Father," he was saying, "forgive them; for they do not know what they are doing" (Luke 23:34).

The words fell like an avalanche of rock upon me and I felt crushed by them. He knew we were the guilty ones, not he—and yet he was offering, or asking, forgiveness for us for what we were doing to him.

None of the other soldiers paid any attention to this. They were busy arguing over who got to keep what clothing, or joining the crowd in reviling and mocking him. I remained silent, troubled. I wanted the whole matter to be over and done with, as quickly as possible. I had been cursed and pleaded with and screamed at from crosses, by men who deserved their fate. But never had I been forgiven. Never had I watched a man suffer unwarranted agony with such an unbowed spirit.

And then it was over. It seemed to be still early, perhaps the middle of the afternoon, but the sun had disappeared behind a strangely overcast sky that brought a heavy darkness and a piercing chill. I was standing at the foot of the middle cross, looking up at the sunken figure of the Galilean, when a final gasp escaped from his body and his tortured breathing ceased. And I could not help but utter aloud a word of acclamation: "Truly, this man was one of the sons of God."

I had come into contact with him for only a few short hours, on the day of his death. I had been a participant in the drama of his dying, as one of the ones who had killed him. And yet I was already feeling that my life was never going to be the same again because of that brief, disturbing encounter.

The memory of his forgiving me especially would not let go of me, though I desperately wanted to forget it. To accept his forgiveness meant acknowledging my guilt, and I fought against that. I had not been responsible—somebody else had made the decision, not me. What could I have done? Nothing.

No. That wasn't so. I was the one in charge. If I knew him to be innocent, might I not have tried to engineer his escape somehow? Then, of course, I would have become the hunted one. I was unwilling to oppose Roman authority for the sake of one innocent man.

So I made my decision by going along. Only much later did I finally come to a genuine decision, beyond the following of orders. Cornelius was the one who helped me take that step—Cornelius, a retired centurion and friend, stationed at Caesarea.

You see, as the years passed and I moved around the eastern provinces from garrison to garrison, I became increasingly aware that a new conviction was growing among some of the people, Jews and non-

Jews alike. My soldiers would bring in to the jail people who had been charged with disturbing the peace, and when I interrogated them I would frequently find them bubbling over about a man named Jesus whom they called Christ and Son of God. And it seemed that nothing could daunt their buoyant spirits. At first I thought it coincidence that the Jesus they were proclaiming had been crucified in Jerusalem. But the more I heard them speak about him—and the more I recalled his calm bearing and disturbing words—the more certain I became: *I* had put to death *their* leader.

But where had they been when he needed them? It was only later, they would explain, that the word had begun to spread like a brushfire that he had really been the Son of God, whose death was overcome by God's powerful love.

I had called him a son of God. They hailed him as *the* Son of God. They meant by that something different, which eventually I came to understand: that this Jesus was God's special envoy to the world, to share the truth of God's forgiving and freeing love to all God's children.

Forgiving! There was that word again. It hadn't freed me. It was torturing me. Cornelius paved the way for me—a centurion in the imperial army, actually coming to believe in the one I had crucified as the Savior of us all (Acts 10—11). It was he who came to me when I was in Caesarea, and told me: "Senecus, his forgiveness *won't* be a burden to you any longer, once you decide to *accept* it. That's when you can become free."

And it was when I decided—finally decided, as a free human being, to join the ragtag band of his followers as one of the worst offenders in need of God's mercy—it was then that what began that bleak day in Jerusalem with a man's dying created in me a new beginning, a new life…a new Senecus.

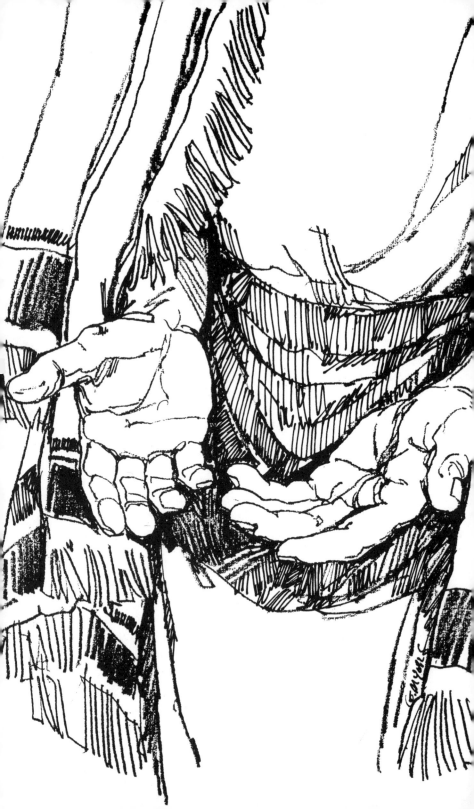

Call Me

Joseph

of Arimathea

(Luke 23:44–56)

Yes, I suppose it took courage to do what I did. But courage was a commodity in rather short supply in most of my behavior. I rose to my position of honor and wealth by playing it safe, carefully weighing consequences, not offending anyone who "mattered." Only there, in the twilight of disaster, in the darkness of hopes dashed, did I finally summon up the nerve to act on my conviction. It was so little—and it was so late. But let me tell you about it.

My name is Joseph, and I am from the Judean village of Arimathea. But early in my successful business career as a tradesman, I moved to Jerusalem, where my fortunes prospered far beyond my wildest dreams. Within two weeks of years, I had risen to such astonishing prominence among the leading men of Jerusalem that I was awarded a seat in the exalted Sanhedrin, the supreme governing council of our people in the city. There I took my place among the priestly aristocracy and the learned scribes as an interpreter of the Jewish law and administrator of justice. Of course, the Romans held ultimate authority, but we remained responsible for managing our own legal affairs and judging the accused under the larger umbrella of Roman order.

My closest friend in the Sanhedrin was a quiet, sensitive man named Nicodemus. It was he who first told me about a young prophet he had met, a certain Jesus Barjoseph, from Nazareth. Having heard stories of this bold preacher and healer, Nicodemus had sought out the man in secret and talked with him. And he came back to share with me the exciting possibility that he had truly been in the presence of the long-awaited Messiah.

He told me of the amazing message this man was spreading about the nearness of the Kingdom of God and the need to make a decision *now* in favor of the Kingdom. He spoke of a remarkable serenity and yet *intensity* in the man as he moved among the crowds that flocked about him. He even declared this Jesus to have some unexplainable power to give wholeness to crippled bodies. And he said that the Nazarene seemed to claim such an unprecedented closeness to God that he dared to offer forgiveness for sins on God's behalf.

"Then why aren't you out there with him?" I asked. "But I can't be absolutely sure that he's really the Messiah," Nicodemus had answered, "—and I don't dare risk myself and my position, if he's not."

Nor did I, even though I pondered the meaning of all that I heard about him, even though I increasingly yearned in my heart to believe, to accept—to become committed to his cause. For centuries, we had been praying to God to send a deliverer. Was it possible that the one we were looking for was truly here among us? But I could not let myself be convinced that it was so.

When he entered Jerusalem that day, I was there among the crowds. But you would not have noticed me. I was hanging back, on the fringes, and I as not dressed in my usual finery. I desperately wanted to see him for myself, but I had to be inconspicuous. It simply would not do for a respected member of the Sanhedrin to be hailing the arrival of a messianic pretender. When the people around me shouted, "Hosanna! Hail to the Son of David!" I wanted to cry out with them. But I kept my silence. I dared not openly show my interest.

Please try to understand the dilemma I was in, before you judge me. My wealth depended upon my good relationships with the rich and the powerful in the community. Through their good graces, I had risen to a position of comfort and status. To come out openly in support of the Galilean meant certain ostracism, a sharp curtailment in business—and certain expulsion from the council. Don't find fault with me for my timidity until you have checked to make sure your own houses are in order. Have you never been guilty of shirking from open allegiance to your Lord when it was "convenient" for you to do so? Have you never taken the easy way out: the deed undone, the mouth clamped shut, when the situation demanded your vigorous response, your strong voice? Yes, my friends, my guilt is not mine alone.

Besides, there was the scandal of that episode in the temple on the very next day. He came storming in and drove out all the people who were doing business there in connection with the buying and selling of sacrificial animals. He wreaked havoc all over the place, and his following was so strong that no one dared stop him. Naturally the priests were greatly upset, and the Sanhedrin was in an uproar over his audacious actions. Many of us were tied in financially with the trade in the temple market, and stood to lose money by his interference. Frankly, I was angry—till Nicodemus cooled me down with a long conversation that lasted late into the night. He finally convinced me of what I should have realized all along—that it was not proper to make a profit off of other people's religious obligations. I felt ashamed that my desire to get ahead monetarily had blinded my spiritual sensibilities. I became more convinced than ever that this was truly an extraordinary individual.

But my fellow leaders were enraged at the brazen upstart from up north, and their fury in the council chamber was intense. They wished to be done with him, and the sooner the better. The people were flocking to the temple to listen to his teaching. The Romans were getting nervous about a possible messianic uprising. So Caiaphas, the high priest and the head of the Sanhedrin, sent a delegation of us to confront Jesus with the crucial question of the authority by which he dared to act and speak as he did.

It was not an easy question to answer, for we, the Sanhedrin, were the defenders of the Law in Jerusalem and he was certainly not acting on our invitation. On the other hand, if he claimed to be acting on the basis of an authority direct from God, he would be laying himself open to possible charges of blasphemy. I was quite unprepared for the skillful way in which he turned the question back on us by demanding that we first tell him by what authority John had baptized—human, or divine? We could not answer that John's authority was from God, for then we had no excuse for not having accepted and followed him. Nor could we say his authority was only his own, for the people revered John as a prophet. My colleagues were on the horns of a very ticklish dilemma, and chose not to answer at all. Inwardly I was delighted. He had outplayed us at our own game.

But the elders in the council were now all the more determined to be rid of a man they increasingly perceived as an enemy to their own religious authority. Nicodemus and I were aware that some kind of plot was brewing. Rumors were afloat that the chief priests had found one of Jesus' followers who was willing to help deliver him into their hands. The stealth was necessary. During the day, he was surrounded by a throng of supporters, and at night we did not know what became of him. It would have to be an inside job.

I was awakened from my sleep early on the morning after the Passover feast with a summons for the convening of the seventy. When I arrived in the council chamber, my heart sank to the pit of my stomach: there he stood. They had arrested him.

I sat mute during the mockery of proceedings that followed, unwilling to risk the displeasure of the overwhelming majority by speaking out in the man's defense. One lackey after another tramped before Caiaphas to offer damaging testimony, but none of them agreed with each other in the details of their testimony. The high priest sought witnesses who would testify that Jesus had committed blasphemy by laying claim to a status of divine sonship, for that would require us to render a verdict of death, by stoning. But he could find none. And when he put the question directly to the accused, Jesus would only say in reply, "It is you who have said this, not I."

It was finally the decision of the Sanhedrin to formulate a charge against Jesus that would enable us to hand him over to the Roman procurator, Pontius Pilate. And the accusation was patently aimed at securing the endorsement of the governor, for it represented a threat against Pilate's own authority: "He claims to be the King of the Jews."

There were those of us in the council who did not consent to this cruel charade, who cringed at the vile insults and physical violence the others heaped on him. But we did nothing to prevent it. And doing nothing was what I was guilty of. I shrank back from the dangers of open acknowledgment of my secret devotion to his cause.

What if I had stood up in the Sanhedrin and declared publicly my support of the Nazarene? Would it have made any difference? Could I have persuaded anyone? I cannot assuage my conscience by contending that it would have been to no avail. What if I had sought him out when I first heard the rumors that they were going to arrest him, and tried to convince him to flee from the city? Would he have done so? I cannot know.

I only know that I was guilty of the sin of passivity, of failing to take a stand when I should have done so. I lived in ardent expectation of the coming of God's reign. I waited longingly for the day when God would establish the sovereignty of divine love among God's people. That was my mistake—I wasn't *doing* anything. I was waiting around for something to happen.

By the time I screwed up my courage and did something, a man had been crucified.

I was in turmoil over my failure of nerve and the hiddenness of my allegiance to the Galilean, and I left the council chamber, left the city—went wandering in the hills around Jerusalem, agonizing over my cowardly hesitancy, struggling with my burning conscience, till the sky became dark and overcast with the threat of a storm. I was heading back toward Jerusalem when I saw the crowd of people gathered on the crown of a hill north of the city gates, a hill called Golgotha. I froze in terror at what was happening there in the murky distance. Golgotha was where the Romans carried out their executions—and I could make out the shapes of three crosses rising above the sea of humanity below.

Numbly I turned and stumbled toward the hilltop in the half-light, as though my feet had a mind of their own. I pushed through the unruly crowd, till I was at the foot of the center cross. I could not bring myself to look up. I didn't have to. I knew.

And in the silent anguish of my grief-stricken spirit, I found myself forming the words: "I believe! Help thou my lack of initiative, my failure of nerve!"

And the stillness was pierced by a gasping voice that said, "It is finished." Then he breathed no more.

In that moment—even when it seemed to be all over, when it would seem prudent simply to let the matter rest—in that moment when there was nothing more to be gained and everything possible to lose, I made up my mind. I would be silent no more. No matter what the cost. No matter how great the risk.

I returned quickly to the city, went straight to Pilate's quarters. Being a member of the high council, I was readily admitted to see him. I stated my purpose without hesitation: I wished to be given the body of the crucified Jesus, that I might bury him in my own rock-hewn tomb.

Pilate was astonished, both that such a one as I should be making the request, and that the person in question was truly already dead. Crucifixions ordinarily took so much longer. But the centurion brought him the news that death had already come. I was granted my request.

There was no possibility of hiding it. The news would be all over Jerusalem by nightfall. But that didn't matter now. I was no longer Joseph the tradesman, carefully weighing and calculating the fruits of my decisions. I was Joseph the disciple, who had finally come out of the shadows into the light.

I had to make haste, so as not to defile the Sabbath, which was near at hand. Back on Golgotha, I set to work with preparations for the burial, only to be interrupted shortly by the arrival of...Nicodemus, my friend, who came bearing spices that he had bought at his own great expense, spices to be used for anointing the body. The two of us wrapped him in a clean linen shroud that I had purchased on the way, and then we carried him to the sepulchre not far away and laid him inside. We closed it up with a large stone over the opening. Several women watched us all the while, and followed at a distance.

That was the extent of what I did. I gave him my tomb to be buried in.

How could I have known that he would have use of it for so short a time?

He was wrong, you know. It wasn't really finished. It was only just beginning.

Performance Notes

These first-person narratives concerning Jesus' birth and death were originally delivered as "dramatic monologues," and the author grants permission for their use in that manner by others. (See the permission statement on the copyright page.) Following are observations that may assist in presenting them.

The first four monologues are appropriate for the four Sundays of the Advent season, and the last six fit the six Sundays of Lent, culminating on Palm Sunday. Other arrangements are possible. The first character I developed was actually John the Baptist, the "forerunner" who is traditionally a focus early in the Advent season. I have placed John's story here after Melchior's, in recognition that both the Magi and the Baptist also properly have a place in the Epiphany season right after Christmas. If you present these during Advent, you should probably portray John as the opening monologue.

I introduced myself afresh each Sunday. That is the reason for the monologue titles. The repeated structure is a way of inviting the listeners to focus their imaginations on the story that is to unfold. The premise throughout is that the congregation is being "visited" by someone from the distant past. He is a guest, who has come for a purpose. With Pontius Pilate, I found myself taking particular liberties in letting him in on what has transpired in the twenty centuries since he issued his deathful proclamation. The other nine demonstrate much more limited knowledge.

You may possess more of a full-blown dramatic flair than I, and decide to go for makeup and the works—especially a suitable variety of beards and wigs. That wasn't my style. I was already leading the worship service, covered from neck to ankles by the Geneva gown. At the appropriate time, I simply turned around, removed my robe, and stood before the congregation again in that character's costume. It was never meant to be anything more than minimally suggestive—to help the mind's eye focus on the character being portrayed.

Few suggestions are given here for costuming. A member of my congregation enthusiastically became my "costume designer" and came up with a wide array of clothing and props. (The eight-foot-tall shepherd's crook for Nathan was my favorite.) You no doubt have someone in your setting who would be delighted to fill that role for you. A local amateur drama group or high school drama club can be of inestimable value to you in helping provide what you need.

I close with some possibly helpful comments about the characterizations as I initially envisioned them.

Ahkmet is wrestling with himself. He's an honest businessman, trying to make an honest living. He wants you to understand that he didn't really do anything wrong, but deep in his heart he knows better. He was too intensely focused on the routine events of life to be open to the unexpected. His excuse is at the very core of these narratives: "If *only* I had known...."

Nathan still has a boyish quality about him, even though he is well grown by the time he delivers his narrative. He is simple and straightforward, and open to the wonder of mystery however bewildering it may be. What especially excites him is that the Messiah is someone he can connect with, in unexpected ways.

Melchior is a dignified personage—not really a "king" but someone who combines learning, wisdom, and social stature. Still, he does not come off as pompous in the least. There is a bit of "life-weariness" about him, but also wariness. (Herod does not fool him for a minute.)

John is rough at the edges. (Burlap conveys that sense well.) His message is intense and demanding, allowing for no compromise. I have made several conjectures with the historical evidence, including the premise that John knew the Essenes well and may even have been one of them for a while. Although Luke portrays John as Jesus' cousin (Luke 1:36), I have focused on John's uncertainty about just who this Nazarene was. Even as the forerunner, John remains one who did not fully comprehend—as the Gospels uniformly point out.

Judas wants to explain his motives. I've never been satisfied with the greed explanation, and to say that

God directed Judas' actions violates the fundamental principle of human freedom and responsibility—which is precisely Judas' anguished cry in *Jesus Christ Superstar*. I have offered an interpretation of Judas' behavior that makes a great deal of sense to me—and it calls attention to how misguided our own allegiance to the Christ can become if we're not careful.

Pilate is an unrepentant voice for the legitimacy of worldly power. He sticks it "in your face," so to speak. (That ridiculous handwashing gesture never fooled anyone.) His defense of his actions culminates in a provocative challenge to those of us today who dare call ourselves Jesus' followers. His brazen posturing is intended to make his hearers squirm uncomfortably in their seats. (I deliberately wore a business suit under my liturgical robe, as the monologue conveys, to set the proper tone for Pilate's mocking stance. You will need to make the monologue's words fit your own choice of apparel.)

Barabbas is a man of violence who is sweating out the imminence of his own execution. He's brusque, blunt. I link him with Simon the Zealot, a legitimate conjecture. The Barabbas I portray is one who has to wrestle in his conscience for the rest of his life over the fact that Jesus took *his* place on the cross. Somehow, his story seemed almost to write itself, taking me in a direction I did not expect when I began.

Simon didn't ask to be thrust onto history's stage. He was picked out of a crowd, at random. How did the church come to remember him by name? Put Romans 16:13 together with Mark 15:21 and you have an inescapable answer. The story I wanted to tell is not just Simon's role in the passion narrative, but how he came to be more than merely a bit player in one act of the drama. The imagined scene with Peter and the other disciples, years laters, completes the puzzle.

Senecus is the one through whose eyes the full drama of Good Friday is disclosed. He is unnamed in the Gospels but his recorded words have become part of the church's witness. I have paraphrased them slightly. (After all, what could a Roman soldier possibly have meant by saying, "This was *the* Son of God"? That was foreign to his tradition.) Because Acts 10—11 narrates the conversion of the centurion Cornelius, I have taken the liberty of joining Senecus' story to his. This monologue is very much about the power and the possibility of conversion.

Joseph is portrayed as one who comes too slowly to a point of conviction and action, and who legitimately berates himself for his play-it-safe cowardice. He wants us to understand his agonizing and indecision, but not to be forgiving too quickly. Through our insight into his vacillation, we come face to face with our own. And even Joseph comes in the end to reflect, "If only I had known...."